WARRIOR TO WHISPERER

An Odyssey into the Quantum Field with Oscar the Cat

Commander Gerald Bunch, US Navy (Ret.)

with Gabriella Gafni

BALBOA.
PRESS

A DIVISION OF HAY HOUSE

Balboa Press books may be ordered through booksellers or by contacting:

Balboa Press
A Division of Hay House
1663 Liberty Drive
Bloomington, IN 47403
www.balboapress.com
1 (877) 407-4847

Because of the dynamic nature of the Internet, any web addresses or links contained in this book may have changed since publication and may no longer be valid. The views expressed in this work are solely those of the author and do not necessarily reflect the views of the publisher, and the publisher hereby disclaims any responsibility for them.

The author of this book does not dispense medical advice or prescribe the use of any technique as a form of treatment for physical, emotional, or medical problems without the advice of a physician, either directly or indirectly. The intent of the author is only to offer information of a general nature to help you in your quest for emotional and spiritual well-being. In the event you use any of the information in this book for yourself, which is your constitutional right, the author and the publisher assume no responsibility for your actions.

Any people depicted in stock imagery provided by Thinkstock are models, and such images are being used for illustrative purposes only. Certain stock imagery © Thinkstock.

Print information available on the last page.

ISBN: 978-1-5043-4932-1 (sc)
ISBN: 978-1-5043-4933-8 (hc)
ISBN: 978-1-5043-4934-5 (e)

Library of Congress Control Number: 2016901006

Balboa Press rev. date: 2/25/2016

ACKNOWLEDGEMENTS

Over the past several years, I have been told several times "You should write a book about what you are doing and how you started doing it." My response had always been the same: "That takes too much time, and I'm too busy." That worked well for me until I met Ms. Gabriella Gafni. Gabriella had been referred to me out of the blue by a former client. She emailed and asked if I would speak with her cats. After doing so, she also told me I should write a book. This time was different because when I said I did not have the time or know how, she immediately responded, "I'll help".

Gabriella is a professional writer who knows the ins and outs of writing, editing and publishing; everything one needs to know about getting a book written. Thus started a professional collaboration and a beautiful friendship. She was not entirely accurate in telling me it would be easy and not take much time, but she was sincere in her desire to have the information contained in this book out in the public domain. For her work, persistence, humor, and deep, abiding compassion, I am eternally grateful.

My editor Ms. Karen Barney has spent many hours in constant discussions with me about how to turn a phrase to make the book a better read. She has a quick mind and a fantastic sense of what sounds right. With her two mega computer screens and lightning-fast typing skills, she saved hours and hours of time and taught me many of the intricacies of word processing.

My good friend Mr. Rex Davis is my computer guru who introduced me to the word processing program used for the book. He also photo shopped several of the pictures in the book. Most importantly, he introduced me to my editor, Karen.

The cover of the book was inspired by the artwork of Ms. Kallaya Boonyasit, of Chiang Mai, Thailand. While on one of our trips there, I bought a painting from her which has served as the inspiration for the cover. She graciously consented to allow me the use of the image. The final cover was designed by graphic artist Ms. Lisa Parker.

Some of the photos of our cats appearing in the book were taken by Ms. Lianne Tauxe. Lianne is a Rescue House volunteer who takes spectacular photographs for the storyboards that are used to explain the background of the cats available for adoption. Her uncanny ability to capture the essence of each cat with her lens has resulted in many cats finding new homes.

Of course, none of this would have ever happened had not Oscar chosen us to be his "forever people". He is the inspiration for the book and my guide and traveling buddy in delving into the mysteries of the quantum field.

For all of the animals with whom I have had the privilege and honor of communicating, I owe a special thanks. It is your willingness to talk with me that has opened my eyes and the eyes of the people with whom you live. We all continue to make a difference in the evolution of life in the universe, one connection at a time.

No list of acknowledgments would be complete without special thanks to my family. My children Trace and Robin have been supportive and encouraging and are a source of such pride for me. As they have grown into their adult years, we have continued to maintain close bonds and to show our love and gratitude for our relationships. They have also graciously allowed me to practice animal communication with their beloved critters, my "grandpets". So thank you Geo, Bailey, Roxy, Sam, Charlie, Holly Berry, Mollie and a number of fish, whose names, unfortunately, I can't remember.

The biggest round of hugs, kisses and thanks go to my wife, Catherine. An accomplished animal communicator herself, she has been instrumental in helping me formulate the words needed to convey the ideas I have presented. Her love, encouragement, patience, and support have been essential in publishing this book.

CONTENTS

FOREWORD

You hold in your hands a fascinating little book that will open your mind and your heart to the interconnectedness of all sentient beings and our natural ability to communicate with each other. When my dog Levi came into my life six years ago, I talked to him incessantly throughout the day. Did he really understand me? His look and often his behavior told me he did. Levi and I began to know and understand each other at a much deeper level than I ever could have imagined.

The more I spoke to Gerald Bunch, my friend and the author of this unique book, about our capacity to communicate with other species, the more it all made sense to me. Not only was my anecdotal experience at play, but so too was that of many others. We humans have a natural tendency to want some evidence, scientific or otherwise, to support our beliefs...our faith. In this book Gerald, a Naval Academy graduate trained in science and engineering, explains in layman's terms the field of "quantum energy" and how we, as sentient beings, "exist as individual quanta of energy in an infinite field of quantum energy". I firmly believe we are all one, all interconnected, and thus all have the ability to communicate with each other. With this book, we finally have the discussion of quantum physics many of us yearn for, to support our belief that we have the ability to communicate with our beloved animals.

From the first chapter about Abe the Cat to a discussion of Quantum Weirdness (Appendix A), you will be hooked. This wonderful and insightful work is a fast read. But be forewarned: set aside time to savor every page because once you start you will not want to put it down. And when you finish, I predict you will be a believer. Have a chat with your cat, a dialog with your dog. Exercise your interconnectedness! As the book points out, this is a path to peace for all sentient beings and a chance to save the planet.

Barry Ladendorf
National President
Veterans for Peace

FOREWORD

"Finally, more out of desperation than cleverness on my part, I began to work with Wesley using language and imagery. ... It seemed pretty far out, but I decided to try. I sat still and began sending thoughts and pictures to Wesley...I also spoke the thoughts out loud ..."

- Biologist Stacey O'Brien -

In my years as a professional animal communicator, I have met my share of skeptics, cynics, believers and everyone in between. As one of the more grounded, 'feet on the ground', psychics, (I have a Master's in Human Behavior), I often surprise people by what I do for a living. It may explain, however, why I find myself in contact with people like Stacy O'Brien (a "CalTech" baby and biologist, who overcame her skepticism and caution about the efficacy of animal communication,) and Gerald Bunch, who not only overcame a deeply ingrained skepticism, but went on to practicing the art of animal communication in his daily life. *Warrior to Whisperer* is his story.

While I can talk about crystals and auras with the best of them, I understand I have to live in the real world. That said, no one would ever accuse me of being 'scientific' or 'mathematical'. Those terms and me, in the same sentence, would be an oxymoron. I certainly didn't have to overcome those 'left brained' stigmas to evolve into the communicator, healer and metaphysician I am. Most of my life I have relied on my natural instinct and empathy. Through my years of communicating with all types of animals I early on started referring to them as each having their own 'canineality, felineality, equineality, aviality, etc., understanding that every animal is sentient and has their own individual 'ality'. Communicating with each of them is as unique an experience as meeting and communicating with new people on a daily basis. That being said, when I first spoke to Gerald and Catherine about tutoring them on their journey, I was delighted to oblige, even though Gerald was up front about his skepticism.

In the ensuing years, I have developed not only a professional relationship with both Gerald and Catherine, and their daughter Trace, but a personal one as well. For this, I am grateful to have the connection with people so clearly open-minded, and hungry for the spiritual knowledge of a journey previously untraveled. As Gerald quotes in the book, "The longest journey is the one between the head and the heart."

With humor and insight, Gerald walks us through his thought processes from being an analytical combat pilot in Vietnam, to being a man who evolves to allow a small little soul, by the name of Oscar, to turn him to mush. Animals have a way of doing that and aren't we blessed for it.

Unflinchingly, he explains to the 'left-brained' people of the world, in quantum theory and with scientific 'proof' as it were, how this elusive practice of animal communication works. Weaving explanations of quantum physics easily back and forth with chapters of examples of his communications, and his process of evolution of thought and belief, he doesn't give anyone a chance to be overwhelmed by either tack, appealing to both skeptics and believers alike.

He goes on to expand on how the special cats in his life, his teachers, have brought him to this spot. Now, it is one of my routine suggestions when speaking to an animal who has anxiety or aggression problems, to ask them to be "Zen Kitty" or "Zen Doggie." or "Zen Horsie." But there are other animals who don't need to be asked. One knows, just by speaking to them, who they are. Gerald's cat, Zen Master Obe Juan, as Gerald refers to him, is one of those special teachers.

Having spoken to Obe Juan over the years, from when he was first adopted, until conversations in spirit after his passing, there was no doubt that he was a teacher. As Gerald describes:

> "In his short time with us, Obe Juan taught us so many lessons...we continue the ongoing journey of living in the now, in a state of gratitude. I am still learning ... I try to pause and ask myself, what would Obe Juan do?"

There are some animals who, when you communicate with them, clearly are advanced souls who have come to this life with a soul contract, just as Obe Juan did with Gerald and Catherine, and just as Oscar has, as well. (For what it's worth, the person who Obe Juan lost in life was waiting for him on the other side, thanking Gerald and Catherine profusely for caring for her furry lost soul.)

In this book, Gerald finds a common ground connecting both left and right brain, to come to the conclusion that all of us, no matter the species, are made of what Neil DeGrasse

Tyson calls "Star Stuff". An astrophysicist, or a combat pilot, may look at this concept in scientific terms. I see that in the metaphysical as 'we are all connected'.

No matter what terms anyone uses, it all winds up the same; we are all the same. We humans, the animals, the earth, the stars, we are all energy, and there is no dividing line between energy. The difference is, when I say it, people might think of it as some sort of "woo woo" explanation without scientific merit. But as is evidenced in *Warrior to Whisperer*, Gerald has bridged that gap to help those who are just like he was years ago to understand in terms they can easily relate to. He does this while sharing a simple and personal journey of love, spirituality and life, but most of all, life with cats. Cats: our greatest teachers.

Lisa Larson, M.A.
Animal Communicator
Carlsbad, California
2015

INTRODUCTION

I am a graduate of the United States Naval Academy, a Vietnam veteran, and a retired career naval aviator. After retirement from the Navy, I had a second career as a commercial airline pilot, during which I flew 747 jumbo jets between most of the major cities of the U.S. and Asia.

I also talk with animals. Notice that I said I talk *with* animals, not *to* them. They talk back to me. We have complete conversations about their likes and dislikes, their problems, and what is going on in their lives.

Nothing in my upbringing in a fundamentalist Christian household, my formal education in engineering and science or my two very technical careers, ever indicated that animal communication would become part of my life. It was not until a little brown tabby cat named Oscar came on to the scene that a dramatic shift in my consciousness began to point me in a new direction. Prior to that, the thought of animal communication would have caused me to roll my eyes and think of the whole concept as delusion, fantasy, or charlatanism — something for a carnival sideshow — and definitely not a part of *real* life.

As I began to learn about animal communication, I was led on a path of discovery that included some serious study of quantum physics. Quantum theory and the resultant quantum physics began to develop in the early twentieth century and has resulted in what many call the second great scientific revolution. While classical Newtonian physics was the basis for the industrial revolution of the eighteenth and nineteenth centuries, the second scientific revolution has resulted in our current lifestyle of cell phones, plasma TVs, and computers. It has also opened the door to explaining phenomena such as animal communication.

From my studies I have learned that all life exists as individual quanta of energy in the infinite quantum field—the basis of our universe. Further, all life forms are intelligent, sentient beings, composed of complex physical, emotional, and psychological makeups, and all emanate from a single source. Each being, or "quanta of energy", is not unlike an individual wave of water in the ocean—each a separate wave, but at the same time a part of the ocean. Each individual, within the multitude of living beings on our planet, is comprised of energy vibrations manifesting as distinct entities. The notion of being separate, however, is an illusion. All of us are integral parts of the whole. We are all expressions of the Divine Mind or Source. This inextricably binds and unifies us in the miracle of being.

As Albert Einstein (1879-1955) stated, "A human being is part of the whole, called by us the universe, a part limited in time and space. He experiences himself, his thoughts and feelings as something separated from the rest, a kind of optical delusion of his consciousness. This delusion is a kind of prison for us, restricting us to our personal desires and to affection for a few persons nearest to us. Our task must be to free ourselves from this prison by widening our circle of compassion to embrace all living creatures and the whole of nature in its beauty."

While the arrival of Oscar in my life prompted the awareness and study of animal communication, prior events and realizations took place that paved the way and launched me on my journey of spiritual awakening. This astonishing paradigm shift occurred as a result of three essential influences. First and foremost was my involvement in Alcoholics Anonymous and the twelve-step program of recovery. This cleared the fog caused by the drug alcohol from my brain and gave me a plan by which to live. It also put me in touch with a higher power. Alcoholics Anonymous (AA) prompted the second major influence, my study of the world's spiritual traditions. From this study, I learned that there are many paths, but only one light. I now realize all humans are essentially the same concerning our hopes, dreams, and fears, and all of us are interconnected. The third influence has been my work with Veterans for Peace, an organization made up of military veterans and their supporters, whose aim is to end war. We humans are much more alike than we are different, and at a core level, all of us want to live peaceful, productive lives of meaning and purpose.

I now believe that I am driven (as are many of my fellow beings) by an evolutionary urge to know and experience Divine Mind. I realize, too, that the Source itself reaches out to become a perfect expression of itself, in, through and as creation. This process has been going on since time immemorial, and will continue. I firmly believe that a full, natural and conscious reconnection between the Source and creation will occur — not in my lifetime probably, but in the natural progression of time and with the evolution of our species.

As an engineering student, a career naval officer, and a commercial airline pilot, I never could have imagined my journey to the point of writing this book. Personal struggle, joy, wonderment, and soul-searching, by turns, paved my path as I went through the experiences of daily living. The process is by no means complete and for that I am most grateful. I have come to realize life is a journey, not a destination, and I eagerly look forward to the new lessons I will inevitably learn as the odyssey continues.

I have many people to thank for help along the way: Eugene Tyc, my mentor, who taught me to appreciate the *is-ness* of life in the now and how not to become entangled in the events of the past or projections of the future; my ex-wife Cinda, who courageously challenged me to be my better self; my children, Trace and Robin, who bring such joy and happiness to me and help me appreciate the continuance of life; Gerald Jampolsky, MD, Eckhart Tolle, Charles Fillmore, Ernest Holmes, Mary Baker Eddy, Deepak Chopra, and many other spiritual leaders and writers who have dedicated themselves to being teachers and exemplars of spiritual living and practice; and last — and most of all — my beloved wife, Catherine, my soulmate and the love of my life, who inspires me on a daily basis with her love, devotion and wisdom, and who has been a major contributor to the writing of this book.

While the people listed have been influential, none of this would have happened without the presence of one beautiful cat named Oscar. He introduced me to a world I had not imaged existed and demonstrated to me the intelligence of non-human life.

As I write, the idea occurs to me that the rather unusual, seeming contradictions of my life's journey were not an accident. They happened according to Divine order, bringing me here, in this time and space, addressing a reading audience. It is my hope that what I have learned will resonate with you and others and make a difference in your awareness of the interconnectedness of all life. If that happens, I will fulfill my mission: to do my best to evolve in this lifetime, and leave the world a better place than I found it — for all of its inhabitants.

CHAPTER 1

COMING HOME

"Gerald, this is Bonnie." (As is the case throughout this book, this is not the real name of the client or the animal.) "Please help me. I'm desperate. Abe left home three days ago, and I can't find him anywhere. He has never done this before. I'm so worried. Can you help me?"

That was the beginning of a phone call I received on a bright, sunny autumn afternoon a few years ago. Bonnie is a woman for whom I had done animal communication several months prior. She lives on the other side of the country from me, and I had never met her or her cats in person, but when operating in the quantum field, time and space are not factors. Physical contact is not required to communicate. She had been referred to me by a friend of a friend because one of her four cats was urinating outside of the litterbox, and another was being a bully to the other cats. At that time, I had connected with her two problem cats, as well as her other cats, one of whom was Abe. The earlier problems were resolved, but now another issue had arisen: Abe had left home.

When I asked her if anything different or unusual was going on in her house, Bonnie told me her son and daughter-in-law had been visiting for the past week. Abe did not seem to like her son at all. As a result, Abe avoided him altogether. She added that her guests were leaving that day, moving to the west coast, and would probably not be back for a long time. She wanted to know if I could contact Abe, tell him that, and ask him to come home.

Lost and runaway animals are the most difficult cases for communicators to handle, and many communicators will not take them. In many cases, the animal has died, and there is nothing that can be done. Sometimes the animal is so lost it doesn't know where it is, so even contacting the animal does not establish where they are or how to direct their guardian to find them. Then there are cases when an animal does not want to be found, has a reason for having left home, and wants to stay away. This seemed to be the case with Abe.

I told Bonnie I would contact Abe and see what was going on with him. Having talked with Abe before, I reviewed my notes and remembered he was a bright and cheery little guy who had an excellent relationship with his cat housemates. It was also clear that Abe dearly loved his person, Bonnie. He was an indoor/outdoor cat, which meant he could come and go as he pleased, but Bonnie always called him in at night. In the past, he had always come home.

I will go into more detail later, but basically to communicate with an animal, I do a short meditation to quiet all of the chatter or "self-talk" in my mind. I also use a photograph of the subject to help me focus on that specific animal. Once I have focused on the animal in question, I begin the conversation. I always start by asking if I may talk to them. After all, most of us humans would not just walk up to someone and start chatting away unless we knew the person we're conversing with fairly well. It's the same with all species. Courtesy, caring, and a slow, relaxed, non-threatening approach are the best ways to establish a rapport. As I communicate, I write down my questions, as well as the answers I receive from the animal.

So I contacted Abe and was relieved to hear from him that he was safe and healthy. Once we established that, I asked him when he intended to go home. I will never forget the sad, plaintive answer of this dear soul. He paused for a moment, and then quietly said, "I don't have a home." I assured him he most certainly did have a home, that Bonnie was very concerned about him and that she was extremely distraught that he was gone. He repeated his earlier assertion that no, he did not have a home. When I asked him why he felt that way he explained because "that person" was there he could no longer live there. I asked him to show me the person who was there. I got a vision of a man of medium height and weight, about five feet nine inches tall and about one hundred sixty pounds, with dark, short hair, medium complexion, wearing jeans and a buttoned shirt. In a later conversation with Bonnie, she said this was an exact description of her son.

Next, I asked Abe if he was lost or if he knew how to get home. He answered that of course he knew his way back to the house. After all, he was an outdoor cat. He had roamed the area many times, and knew his way around. I then asked him if he had enough food and water. He told me he did, and that he had been getting food at the house of friendly human. I asked him to show me the house, and I got a vision of a white house with blue shutters and a fence around the yard.

Having established that he was safe, well fed, and knew where he was, I told him that the person he did not like was no longer with Bonnie. I informed him the person had left and would not be back. I let him know his home was there, his cat friends were all there, and that Bonnie truly loved him and wanted him to come back. He seemed hesitant to accept all of this, so I asked him if he would be willing just to go to the house, stay outside, and check it out. He told me he would think about it. I again told him how much he was missed, how much Bonnie loved him, and how worried she was. In my experience, animals like to be told how much they are loved over and over again. Then again, isn't that true of humans too? I said my goodbyes and closed the connection.

I called Bonnie and reported the conversation to her, reading my transcript word for word. She confirmed the description of her son and said she was pretty certain she knew the house where Abe was being fed. She assured me she would keep an eye out for him. I only had to wait about three hours for an update. "Guess who just came up to the house!" Bonnie exclaimed with a combination of joy and relief in her voice. "Abe is back!" About an hour after that I received an email with a picture of Abe lying on Bonnie's lap.

So, how did all of this happen? By formal education, I am an engineer. The idea of communicating with a different species on the other side of the country is something I would never in a million years have thought possible when I completed college and started my career. I have learned many things in the years since I graduated from the Naval Academy and flight school and subsequently went to war. I never thought I would learn that all life forms are intelligent, sentient beings with complex lives, thoughts, and emotions. I never imagined it could be possible to communicate with all life forms through the zero-point energy of the quantum field. I certainly never thought that it would be possible for me to do that on a regular basis.

How does animal communication work? Well, how it works doesn't matter nearly as much as the fact that it *does* work. It is also worth noting that this is not a unique "gift" given to a few anointed ones. The ability to communicate with other species is a capability with which we are all born. As we learn spoken language, this ability retreats to the back of our consciousness where, for most humans, it lies dormant. However, animal communication remains a capability all humans can re-learn, and anyone can master.

Later in the book I will write about how I learned to communicate and how it works, but again, the how is not as important as knowing it does work. To draw a parallel, one would not have to go too far back in history to the time when flipping a switch on the wall to illuminate a room would have been viewed as black magic. Even now, most people do not know how that works. They just know it does, and it happens every time they flip that switch.

I have the same feeling about animal communication. Through my brief look at quantum physics, the quantum field and the zero-point energy of the quantum field, I am beginning to understand the science behind animal communication. However, I know from experience that I don't need to know *how* it works, I just need to know that it *does work*, and it works all the time.

In a sense, like Abe, I, too, am coming home. I am coming home to a way of thinking and being in the world I did not know was ever a part of me. Likewise, perhaps the entire human race is coming home to a fuller appreciation of the other species with whom we share our planet, these other species with whom we exist in the quantum field.

CHAPTER 2

A THUNDERBOLT
NAMED OSCAR

In the autumn of 2008, a few years before the conversation with Abe, a series of events transpired which resulted in an extremely sudden, unexpected paradigm shift for me. A new reality began to reveal itself, and I had the first whispers of a feeling that my life would never be the same.

It all started one memorable Friday afternoon when my daughter Trace called me from the school where she taught. She is a volunteer with a local organization called "The Rescue House" (a feline rescue and adoption agency) and has been a cat person all of her life. The Rescue House, a non-profit, all-volunteer organization co-founded by Joan Star, has been in operation since 1999, and to date has saved more than eleven thousand felines.

Although I knew about The Rescue House and we had briefly sheltered a cat once before, the notion of "bonding" with other species had never entered my thoughts. From my perspective, animals were purely instinctual entities, devoid of intellectual, emotional, or psychological substance. Throughout my life, I was benignly indifferent to animals, experiencing neither much affection nor antipathy for them.

While growing up, there were always a number of animals around me (dogs, cats, goats, chickens, etc.). However, they were in the periphery of my awareness, and I certainly never thought about the possibility of their sentience, let alone their ability to communicate...but I'm getting ahead of myself.

Back to that unforgettable September afternoon. Gary, the custodian at Trace's school, brought her a young cat that had been wandering around the school grounds. Searching the neighborhood around the school, Trace was unable to find anyone who knew the cat, or where he might live. With no other option, she decided to get him into The Rescue House system. It being late on Friday, her choices of what to do with a stray cat were quite limited. She tried to find a foster home for him in the system, but she was unsuccessful in locating a sanctuary for the little orphan. This young feline had no idea of what life had in store for him; or, on second thought, perhaps he did. Trace asked whether my wife Catherine and I could take the cat, estimated to be about five months old, just for the weekend. "If you can't," she said, "I'll have to keep him locked in the supply room at school until I can find a foster home for him."

Catherine and I agreed, and Trace brought the cat, named "Gary" in homage to his original rescuer, to our house. From the moment the tabby came in, I thought he was one of the most engaging, friendly creatures that I had ever encountered. I began to refer to him as "a cog" – a dog in a cat's body. He spent the afternoon exploring, playing, and endearing himself to us in the most natural, delightful manner. Later that night, he lay on my lap and stretching out his paws, looked very much like he had already made himself right at home. As he arched his back, I rubbed his belly and told him, "You look like a little hot dog." Instantly, the famed jingle came to mind: "… If I were an Oscar Mayer Wiener, everyone would be in love with me." That was our homeless guest – a bundle of love. We immediately dispensed with the name "Gary", and replaced it with our private label for him, "Oscar". After all, he was only going to be with us for a few days, so what did it matter?

During his weekend stay with us, Oscar enchanted us with abundant displays of cuteness, attention, and affection. At times, when my eyes met with those of the little fur ball, it seemed as if I could almost sense his intelligence, emotions, and sentience. Then my logical, left-side brain would kick in, and I would tell myself, *What am I thinking? He's only a cat!* In those few days together, though, he completely obliterated my false perception of cats and their reputation of being aloof, disinterested, and uncaring toward the human race. He looked at us with what appeared to be such awareness and connection that it almost seemed he wanted to communicate with us.

Trace had told us that on Monday "Gary" had a veterinary appointment to be examined, neutered and micro chipped. One of the local vets, who donates time to The Rescue House on an 'as available' basis, would perform the procedures. The protocol is to bring a cat in first thing in the morning and drop him/her off. As the day unfolds, the vet performs any and all necessary procedures whenever time permits. Since Trace had to work, she asked if Catherine could take Gary to the vet. Catherine agreed so on Monday morning she took him to the vet's office and left him with the very busy receptionist, saying only, "Here's the cat from The Rescue House. Someone else will pick him up this afternoon."

Later that day, when the procedures were over, Trace informed me over the phone, "Gary is ready. I'll bring him to your house."

"Oh, you mean Oscar!" I said with somewhat of an amused tone.

"Why are you calling him that?" Trace asked in a very surprised voice.

My daughter laughed when I told her our story of how we had named Oscar, and she proceeded to recount what at the time appeared to be an incredible tale. Apparently the vet technicians, after seeing our new friend sitting up on his hind legs swatting at a toy on a string, decided that he looked like a boxer working a speed bag. Not having heard a name for their little patient, they called him "Oscar", after the prizefighter Oscar de la Hoya. At that time, the anecdote seemed to be nothing more than a humorous coincidence, and we jokingly said, "Oscar has named himself." Since then, however, I have come to believe that there are no coincidences in life. Everything happens in Divine Order. There is no doubt in my mind that Oscar deliberately told us his name.

On Tuesday morning, Trace called to say that she had found a foster home for Oscar, and she would come by and retrieve him that night. I had to attend a Home Owner's Association meeting and planned to leave before Trace came over. As I prepared to go, I looked at the little being at my feet, and said casually, "Goodbye, little cat! It has been such fun having you here. You're such a sweetheart."

I climbed into my car and had not gone more than a mile or two down the road when I was hit by an emotional thunderbolt that permeated every fiber of my being. Pulling over to the side of the road, I felt such deep emotion that I was moved to tears. I called Catherine on my cell phone, and almost in a tone of desperation, choked out the words, "Don't let Trace take Oscar! He has to stay with us!"

After a measured pause, I heard Catherine say, "Are you serious? You know we can't keep a cat. We travel too much!"

A few years prior to this I had retired as a commercial airline pilot. Catherine had also retired from her career as a psychotherapist. Since then we'd been engaging in our passion to travel and learn about the cultures and spiritual traditions of the world. We had intended to continue traveling and living out of a suitcase for much of our lives. The kids were grown and gone and all of the plants in our condo were artificial. Whenever someone would ask me why I had no pets, I would answer in my somewhat salty navy language with, "I don't want to own anything that shits, sheds or eats."

Unbeknownst to us, however, our lives were about to unfold in a direction we had never anticipated. In short, the universe had other plans for us, and Oscar was to play a significant role in them.

"I know we travel too much and we can't keep a cat," I replied, "and I don't know how we are going to do it, or even why I'm saying this, but he has to be with us."

"Let's discuss this when you come home," Catherine said.

"OK," I answered, "but just don't let Oscar go right now." Somehow, I had an inner knowledge that there was really nothing to discuss.

OSCAR

CHAPTER 3

THE WARRIOR

One of my fond memories of growing up was listening to the radio program "The Lone Ranger". Every night the announcer would start the program by saying: "Now, let us return to those thrilling days of yesteryear..." With that in mind, I'm going to return to my yesteryears for some background.

Very early on one hot, muggy tropical morning in 1968, I sat in my aircraft on the flight deck of a U.S. Navy aircraft carrier, about to fly my very first combat mission. The Viet Cong had just launched the infamous Tet Offensive, designed to expel the United States from Southeast Asia, once and for all. Rivulets of sweat streamed down the back of my neck. Was it the humid weather, fear of combat, or just the normal tension that goes along with all flight deck operations? I had no time to speculate as to why because after another moment of watching the dawn sky lighten, it was time to get to work.

Heeding the gestures of the flight deck director, I took my turn and taxied onto the "cat". This is Navy slang for the catapult, a mechanical device just beneath the flight deck used to accelerate an aircraft to launch speed. When launched, my airplane would be rocketed from zero to one-hundred-eighty miles per hour in just 2.5 seconds. Reaching that velocity, I would be hurled out from the ship into the rapidly lightening sky.

On the catapult, after my weapons were armed, I received the signal to run the engines to full throttle. I did so, performed a final instrument check, and leaned back against the head restraint. This is done to avoid the impact of eleven g's of force at the firing of the cat. I then saluted the launch officer, and I was off for two hundred fifty-one feet of wild acceleration —what we pilots in the squadron called the best ride in the world.

After the launch, when airborne, it took a second or two to refocus my eyes and get my brain working again. Raising the landing gear, I accelerated and began to climb to altitude while raising the flaps. I got my navigation bearings, put my full focus on my mission, and headed for the coast of North Vietnam.

When flying to a target, going through a wall of flak, or landing on an aircraft carrier, it is absolutely necessary to stay completely focused on the task at hand. The brain must be compartmentalized, maintaining an airtight thought processes, incapable of deviation from the sole objective: to execute the job of flying the airplane.

As I discovered during my intensive psychological screening for combat aviation, some people have a greater ability to compartmentalize (i.e. seal off their thoughts and feelings) than others. While attempting to land a high-performance jet on the pitching and rolling deck of an aircraft carrier, a Navy pilot cannot be thinking of his wife and kids at home or whether the new coach will bring his favorite team to that year's Super

Bowl. He must concentrate solely on the job at hand and devote his full abilities to complete the task.

As I think back now, I realize that it probably was easier for me to contain my emotions and compartmentalize my thoughts than for many others, given how my life had evolved to that point. For most of my life, I had lived in a state of cognitive dissonance. My experiences, thoughts, and emotions were always in conflict, and I felt as if I were constantly walking on eggshells. The dysfunctional nature of my early family life (characterized by unrecognized and unnamed alcoholism, emotional and, to some extent, physical abuse) was masked by outward "conventionalism". There was a perpetuated myth that we were all "one big, happy family". Any reaction that did not further support that mythology was derided or ignored. As a result, I learned to submerge my feelings, put on a happy face, and stuff my emotions.

I was born and raised in rural Virginia, on the outskirts of Washington, D.C., before the area was engulfed in urban sprawl. While in high school, I enlisted in the Naval Reserve, then applied for and won an appointment to the Naval Academy. I studied engineering for four grueling years, graduated in the middle of my class, and was commissioned to be an ensign in the U.S. Navy. The day after graduation I married my first wife Cinda, whom I had met in high school and dated while in college. A month later I reported to flight school in Pensacola, Florida. Fifteen months after that I reported to my first squadron in San Diego, California. With my recently earned naval aviation "wings of gold", a wife, our two dogs, and soon thereafter, our first daughter, Trace, I was ready to take on the world.

When I first flew off to war, never in my wildest dreams could I have imagined that, at some later point in my life, I would come to think about my fellow human beings on planet Earth in a significantly different way. Nor in any of those wild dreams could I possibly have conceived of the idea of communicating with other species, establishing connections of the heart and soul that would forever change me.

CHAPTER 4

THE JOURNEY BEGINS

It's a long way in space, time, and consciousness from that moment on the aircraft carrier, as I waited for a launch to make war on my fellow human beings, to being aware of the universal oneness of all life. How did I get from there to here? To quote a Native American proverb, "The longest journey is the one between the head and the heart".

I started this book as an animal communicator, followed by an introduction to Oscar, then a brief description of my warrior days. A lot happened between the time I thought of myself as a "hot shot" Navy pilot and when Oscar rocked my world and changed my life. Therefore, I thought it might be useful share some of the crucial events that occurred on that long path from there to here.

The year 1972 marked the beginning of profound personal growth and change. It was the year I got sober. At that time Cinda and I lived in San Diego with our two girls, Trace and Robin, and I continued to serve as a Navy pilot. At the Naval Academy drinking was strictly forbidden, but upon graduation from school I began to drink on a regular basis. Over the years, my drinking had steadily progressed and worsened. I drank more often and more heavily, with less and less predictability. My career choice gave me an opportunity to further my addiction. At that time, the Navy encouraged close camaraderie with lots of parties and "beer busts". When I was shore-based, I drank almost every day at home and work, sometimes less, but mostly more. On some days, I would drink myself to sleep at night and be so hung over the next day that I would swear never to drink again. Inevitably, after a day of no alcohol the cycle began again. In those days, I was unaware of the term "functional alcoholic". As I look back now, I see that's exactly what I was during that time. I was able to perform sufficiently at my job while engaging in behaviors for which I was in persistent denial. I told myself numerous times that I was going to cut back or quit, but the simple truth was that I could not. I always went back to drinking.

In April 1972, I went to a Friday night party with friends. Anticipating the inevitable, Cinda opted to work the night shift, so as not to be around me when I came home. That night, I drank until I blacked out and didn't even know how I managed to get home. Having reached the end of her emotional rope, Cinda confronted me two days later when I had sobered up. Her words forever changed my life. "I am not going to stay here and watch you kill yourself," she told me. "If you don't go to Alcoholics Anonymous, I'm leaving you and taking the kids." Only later did I come to realize how courageous she was to take that stand and make that statement. But at the time I was deeply and self-righteously upset, in total denial of any problem, and determined to prove her wrong.

A neighborhood friend of ours had children who were the same age as our girls. As the kids became friends and played together, she observed what was going on at our house. Our neighbor attended a program called Al-Anon, a support group for family and friends of alcoholics. One day, she told Cinda about Al-Anon and invited her to attend a meeting. Cinda agreed and, at her first meeting, she met a man named "Bill" (not his real name), who also was an alcoholic, but was attending Al-Anon that day as well. After speaking with Cinda for a while, Bill offered to speak with me and gave her his phone number. Cinda passed the number on to me, saying, "You need to talk to this Bill fellow." *This will be easy*, I told myself.

I called Bill, thinking I would make an appointment for a week or two from then, and by that time, the whole matter would be forgotten. Luckily for me, though, Bill would not be put off. He said he would come right over, and within twenty minutes there was a knock at the door. Fulfilling all my misconceptions about what an alcoholic looked like, there he was, a disheveled looking older man complete with a beat-up pickup truck behind him in my driveway. I was certain that he and I had nothing in common. I invited him in, sat down to "listen", and was ready to be completely condescending. However, Bill was very rational and calm and addressed me in an unassuming, non-judgmental manner. He quietly told me about his life, past and present. Although I'd been prepared to discount him, I realized that his story was similar to mine, not in terms of particular events, but rather in the way in which his drinking had progressed. He described the emotional and spiritual downward spiral of out-of-control drinking in which I saw my life proceeding.

The truth was that I wanted to quit, but I could not control my addiction. Since that day I've learned that alcoholism is a genetic disease, passed down through generations. Members of alcoholic families with this genetic predisposition will, almost invariably, succumb to the condition, if exposed to sufficient quantities of alcohol. Since my father, grandfather, and numerous uncles were alcoholics, genetics certainly played a role in my circumstances. At that crucial moment, however, I had no inclination to think about reasons or causes. I needed help and, somehow, deep inside, I knew that I had to change my life.

Chinese philosopher Lao Tzu has been credited by many as saying "A journey of one thousand miles begins with a single step." In my case, the journey started with twelve steps.

The night after my conversation with Bill, I attended my first AA meeting. Over time, as I remained in the program, I discovered the invaluable lessons of the 12-Step Program which, in a nutshell, involved the following suggestions: (1) admitting to myself and others my powerlessness over alcohol (2) developing a reliance on a higher power, greater than myself – however I conceived of God or the Source; (3) defining my personal interpretation of God, and deferring to that power for sustenance; (4) taking a moral inventory of myself; (5) admitting to the higher power, myself, and another human being the exact nature of my wrongs; (6) surrendering to the inevitability of change and accepting responsibility for it; (7) facilitating change through meditation and alignment with spiritual principles; (8) assessing the extent of harm caused by my alcoholism and discerning to whom I should or should not make amends (i.e., asking myself whether an apology would only cause further injury to specific individuals); (9) making amends to the appropriate people, taking care not to do further harm; (10) continuing to take moral inventory and when I made mistakes, promptly admitting them; (11) reflecting and awakening to the presence of God or the Source as I understand

"It" to be; and (12) giving back to the community — to individuals in similar circumstances or with other addictions, and keeping on the track of self-improvement.

In my opinion, many of the principles which are the basis of the above steps can be integrated into virtually anyone's life. By internalizing the twelve steps over a period of time, I engaged in a process of self-discovery and empowerment that I had never before experienced.

CHAPTER 5

THE JOURNEY CONTINUES

My consciousness-shift expanded even further when Cinda and I began to attend the Christian Science Church of which our neighbor was also a member. This study of new thought spirituality aided me in connecting with the Divine Mind from a metaphysical perspective. This was entirely different from my previous beliefs, the so-called "traditional" Christian perception of "God, the Father". I had visualized God as a bearded old man, seated on a cloud, presiding over the universe and passing judgment on our activities.

As a student of Christian Science, I studied with Eugene Tyc, a man whom I deeply admired. I also read voraciously, and was impacted by such new-thought visionaries as Charles and Myrtle Fillmore, Deepak Chopra, Ernest Holmes, Mary Baker Eddy, and countless others. The message imparted by all of these teachers was fundamentally the same: that we are all one. We are interconnected with the Divine Mind that is the basis of all intelligence in the universe. Furthermore, all sentient life has individual equal access to that intelligence and love.

While my spiritual studies continued, my Navy career progressed and I eventually found myself as an instructor pilot in Pensacola, Florida. With more regular hours and a set routine, I was able to attend night school. By the time I transferred to my next duty station, I had earned a Master's Degree in Public Administration.

My next set of orders involved sea duty and took me far from home for extended periods of time. As a consequence, my marriage suffered. Two years of marriage counseling revealed that Cinda and I were not suited for each other as a couple — a fact I had inherently understood, but never actually stated, even to myself. Due to that understanding, my desire to remain in the Navy, and Cinda's reluctance to be subjected to further transfers, we ultimately parted. To ensure the balance and continuity of their lives, the girls lived with me, but Cinda and I officially had joint custody. We remained friends (as we are to this day), coming together as parents to make decisions regarding our girls.

During this time of intense reflection and change, I found myself in a bookstore one day, staring at a book entitled *Love Is Letting Go of Fear* by Gerald G. Jampolsky, MD. I had no idea what the book was about or even why it attracted me, but I knew I had to have it. It was another momentous milestone on my life's journey. Upon reading Dr. Jampolsky's book, I learned that by making changes to my thoughts and attitudes, I could experience a life of inner peace, not dependent upon outward circumstances. By focusing on my outlook on life, I could have an influence on what went on in my day to day living. I was to learn much more about the power of intention when I started a serious study of quantum physics. At the time, even this simple concept, that we have a measure of influence over how things manifest in our lives, was astounding to me.

With these ideas and feelings germinating in my soul, a metamorphosis began to take place within me. I became more introspective, more aware of my emotions, and more expressive. I also read more, and continued therapy sessions. Fascinated by the study of the human mind and behavior, I entered a Master's program in Counseling Psychology at a local university. Little did I know what a significant change would occur in my life's path. It was there, in graduate school, that I met my soulmate. Her name was Catherine.

Friends and classmates for six months, we dated for the next six and discovered we had many intellectual and spiritual commonalities. I didn't plan to fall in love. However, as I have discovered so many times in my life, when I follow my "gut feeling" (or, as I have come to understand it, Divine guidance), my life path unfolds in a beautiful and wondrous manner.

In 1985, Catherine and I graduated with our Master of Arts degrees in Counseling Psychology. I requested an assignment to the position of Director of the Alcohol Rehabilitation Center and Family Services Center in Pearl Harbor, Hawaii. The Navy concurred, and I moved to the Islands, soon followed by Catherine. Six months later, we were married at the Unity Church in Honolulu, where we were active members. Although we would have welcomed the girls into our home, they decided to remain in California with their Mom, to further maintain the continuity of their lives with high school and friends.

After three more years in the Navy (in which I served a total of twenty-eight years, including enlisted time and time at the academy), I retired at age forty-five. I considered a civilian career in counseling but then discovered that commercial airline pilots had recently prevailed in an age discrimination lawsuit against their employers. I was no longer considered too old to begin a career with an airline company. *At this age, I can still fly, and become a counselor when I retire from the airline,* I thought. So, I applied to several airlines and was eventually hired as a pilot by Northwest Airlines, a job that I held for the next eighteen years.

As I started my career at Northwest, I discovered that the union to which I now belonged, the Air Line Pilots Association, along with the Federal Aviation Administration, and my new employer, Northwest Airlines, had a joint program designed to identify pilots suffering from alcoholism. The purpose of the program was to offer treatment for the disease and return pilots to duty. With fifteen years of sobriety, a Master's degree in Counseling Psychology, and several years of experience directing a treatment program with the Navy, acting as the union representative for the airline program seemed to be a perfect fit. I welcomed the opportunity to give back and share my personal and professional knowledge, so I volunteered to be the union leader of the program. I continued to fly and did the union work on a volunteer basis in my spare time.

As a commercial airline pilot, my desire to travel and continue to learn about the world met with an ideal career opportunity. This enabled me to discover, explore and delve into different cultures, belief systems and ways of living that were new to me. I did not know it at the time, but I was adding building blocks to my awareness of the "oneness of all life".

CHAPTER 6

SAME DIFFERENCES

I grew up in what I thought at the time was a conventional family. One of the lessons continually imparted to me, in various ways, was that our way was the "right" way and therefore, other people's ways were "wrong". In fact, many other people's ways were considered to be "wrong", "bad", and definitely inferior. These deeply entrenched beliefs may have been the result of religion, race, or ethnicity. The reality was that they were my beliefs and not only did I have a lot to learn, I also had a lot to unlearn.

When I got sober, I came face to face with Step 2 of the 12- Step program of Alcoholics Anonymous, which states in part, the need "…to believe in a power greater than ourselves". Deep within, I realized that I did not fully accept the traditional God of my upbringing. Soon after I started in AA, I began to attend the Christian Science Church, and over the years also studied at Unity Church and the Church of Religious Science. The so-called "new thought" religions taught that God is not a separate being, apart and different from us. They taught we are all part of a unified whole, and are individualized expressions of God the Source.

The concept was easier for me to grasp when it was explained that we are all like waves in the ocean. Each of us is individual and unique, but we are all part of the vast ocean. In his book *The Great Work of Your Life: A Guide for the Journey to Your True Calling*[ii], author Stephen Cope paraphrases from the Bhagavad Gita, the ancient spiritual text of the Hindu religion. "The self (and here we mean the small "s" self, which is our current form and personality) is described as a wave. We're all familiar with the action of the wave: The wave rises in the sea and, having arisen, appears to have its individual form, to be a 'thing in itself'. In fact, however, the wave is always and everywhere one with the sea. It arises from and returns to the sea. It is made of the same stuff as the sea. It is the sea in every way. Indeed, even in the fullness of its apparent individual being—its apparent individual 'wave-ness'— it is never really other than the sea." From my further study of quantum physics, I now realize that we are all quanta of energy in the vastness of the quantum field. I came to believe the ocean or quantum field is analogous to that Higher Power that many people call God.

These realizations were coming to me while I was continuing my Navy career, serving in that organization that used the recruiting phrase, "Join the Navy and see the World". Little did I know how much of the world I was yet to see. My naval service was followed by my airline career, during which I flew to many of the major cities of the world on an ongoing basis.

Writing about waves in the ocean or quanta of energy in the universe is all well and good, but I needed proof; I wanted to experience this "oneness" myself. And so I evolved as a "people watcher". One of my favorite things to do, when

I traveled, was to observe people in their daily activities. It could be a busy street in New York, a sidewalk café in Paris, a public park in Istanbul, or a small village in Bali. I spent hours and hours just watching people live their lives. The families, the couples, the kids playing, and, of course, everyday people interacting with each other. I spent hours going to museums and cultural displays and events. I also spent just as many hours going into grocery stores or local outdoor markets to see what was on the shelves or in the stalls and to see how people did their shopping.

During this period of growth and change, it became increasingly apparent to me that respect for cultural diversity involves acknowledgment of oneself as "the other". The farther I went from my home, the more I came to realize the essential similarities of all life. Not only are we "in" the universe, all wavelets in the ocean or quanta of energy in the quantum field, but we "are" the universe/ocean/quantum field. In truth, we are all one and the same, and our apparent differences are only on the surface. I have a T-shirt that has the word "eracism" on the front, a combination of the words "erase" and "racism". On the back of the shirt are the words "There is only one race. It is human. Everything else is culture." I have come to believe that there are no truer words than those.

As I traveled and observed, I came to realize that while there is great truth in the phrase "everything else is culture", there can be great differences in cultural norms that can be quite striking. In Japan, I observed that loud, attention-grabbing behavior of any kind is abhorrent to the Japanese people. With a well-deserved reputation for politeness, the Japanese do not condone loud, irreverent behavior amongst themselves. A traditional greeting between people is done by placing the hands at one's side, and bowing at the waist to the other. The back-slapping "hail fellow, well met" camaraderie of the Western culture is at distinct odds with this custom. However, beneath this surface difference, the reality is that in both cultures, people want to greet, acknowledge each other, and get along.

In Thailand, home to those who, in my opinion, are among the gentlest individuals on the planet, greetings are also very different than what we are used to in the United States. On my first trip to Bangkok with Northwest Airlines, I observed our Thai crew members greeting their families and friends with the 'wai' gesture. This is done by placing their palms and fingers together, as in prayer, raised to the level of their faces, accompanied by a slight bow (In Thailand, the McDonald's restaurants have a statue of Ronald McDonald out front in the 'wai' posture.). These fundamental practices may *appear* to be different as one travels geographic distances, but their meaning is identical. The handshake, the bow, or the 'wai' are all forms by which we humans greet each other. I gradually came to the realization that while specific cultural behaviors may differ, the intentions have a universality that speaks to our deepest similarities as human beings on planet earth.

For Northwest Airlines, Tokyo was a major hub airport in Asia, and almost every trip went through Narita, the airport serving Tokyo. Located about thirty miles outside of Tokyo, our crews always stayed at the same hotel in the small city of Narita. I stayed there so often that I eventually purchased a motorbike that I parked behind the hotel. In my off hours, I would frequently go for rides in the countryside, far from our hotel. The further I rode from the hotel, the fewer Japanese people I encountered who spoke any English at all; but as it turned out, that didn't matter. It was just a wonderful experience to ride along, stop for a meal or a snack, and communicate by nodding and using my few significant words: "konichiwa" (good afternoon) and "domo arigato" (thank you very much). The fact that I made an effort at all was appreciated by my hosts. In Bangkok, a city as large as New York, I was amazed at the number of Buddhist temples I saw. The overwhelming feeling of devotion the Thai people have for their faith was almost palpable. Buddhism is a part of daily life for most of the Thais, and for us, as guests in their midst, we could feel the sense of serenity and calm of so many of the people.

On a trip to India, I noticed that men and women refrained from touching each other in public, either by way of a greeting or a display of friendship. In fact, men and women rarely travel in each other's company, unless as a family. Also, adults would never touch children on the head. While we Americans may consider this to be a pleasant gesture connoting fondness, the gesture is considered inappropriate in India.

During another trip to India with Catherine, we were on a guided tour. In one of the remote villages in the center of the country, we enjoyed a delicious meal at the home of a potter, our tour guide's friend. Dinner was cooked on a wood burning stove, while we sat on the dirt floor of his hut, feeling completely at home. Our families spent the evening singing songs, laughing, and talking about life and family. It was one of the simplest, yet most memorable nights of all of our travels. We were about as far as apart as two cultures could be and yet we felt as close and connected with this family, who we had just met, as if we had known them for years. We humans all have universal feelings of love, caring for family, friends, and enjoying one another's company and those feelings were so very evident to us that night.

For all of the cultural difference and similarities that I experienced, there were instances when I encountered genuine cultural clashes. Australia was also a favorite place Catherine and I liked to visit. There we learned about the Aboriginal peoples, whose ancestors were indigenous to the continent. We visited the town of Alice Springs and from there drove to Uluru, known to westerners as "Ayers Rock". Uluru is a large sandstone monolith that rises hundreds of feet above the surrounding flat desert. It is a spectacular sight and is a sacred place for the Aboriginal people, who specifically ask that people not climb on it. Tourists (both foreign and local Australians), often ignore that request, and climb to the top just for the sake of the accomplishment. What one culture views as a sacred place to honor, another sees as a challenge to conquer. Catherine and I decided that we would respect the wishes of the Aboriginal people and not climb to the top. We felt that it was enough just to stand there and feel the energy of this sacred spot.

I recount these various examples of my cultural education to point out how I came to the belief that we are all one, sharing the same hopes and dreams, loves and fears. We want our families to be safe, we want food and shelter, and we want to be acknowledged. We laugh and cry at the same things because, at the most fundamental level, we are the same. We are one.

As my worldview shifted, and I became more involved as a peace activist, I joined the organization Veterans for Peace. Among other readings, I have studied the books and attended lectures of Paul Chapell, a West Point graduate, Iraqi war veteran and peace activist. He makes a compelling case of how we humans are not naturally violent toward each other and, in fact, have to be 'programmed' to be able to go to war. Our political leaders do this by convincing us that the 'enemy' is some 'other', 'lesser' and 'sub-human' species. We naturally find it difficult to make war on and kill our fellow humans. However, if we are taught to call them by denigrating names, or label them as aggressors, or just plain bad guys, then we're able to overcome our natural inclinations toward non-aggression and are able to make war on "them".

The idea that the "other", "lesser", or "evil one" was so very different from me was part of my belief system for many years, especially during my military service. I have since come to understand otherwise. While exploring different cultures and customs, I continued my spiritual studies and spent part of every day in meditation. I experienced a slow, gradual development of the idea that 'otherness' did not exist and that there is never an enemy, only the manifestation of myself in others.

I could never have imagined that one of my most influential teachers would be a being of a different species, with four legs and wrapped in a tabby-colored fur coat. My traditional Christian upbringing taught me that humans were to have dominion over all the animals of the earth. This idea is based on the premise that one species, humans, is superior to the others. When we dispense with hierarchical notions, we receive the greatest, most beautiful surprise: the awareness of the fundamental equality and oneness of all life. All life is valuable. All life belongs in the universe. As humans, we think of ourselves as different from other humans, due to nationality, culture, language or skin color. When thinking about or perceiving different species, we view ourselves as different due to instincts, intelligence, emotions, body shape, lifestyle or lifespan. The reality is that we are all part of the one great life force expressing the Divine in a myriad of ways. All life forms have intelligence, sentience, and purpose. Imagine reaching beyond the veil of presumed differences to access what some of those other life forms have to say!

CHAPTER 7

BRIDGING REALMS
OF CONSCIOUSNESS

Traveling and having enjoyable interactions with people from different cultures expanded my perspective and awareness that there are many ways of "being" in the world. Having been exposed to such differences – and sameness – I now realize this was the prelude to a transition into yet another realm of consciousness: that of animals, and specifically, felines. Sometimes each step of the journey known as life seems to be a well-calculated and known progression, but sometimes it calls for a leap of faith. I have come to believe that Divine guidance is always available to each of us, but we have to learn how to listen for it and recognize it. In much the same way as I had to adjust when traveling to different countries, learning new gestures, languages, and cultures, I also had to be introduced and adapt to the World of Oscar.

During my childhood, a cat or two had always been around our house, but never indoors, only outside and on the periphery of my life. During my first marriage, Cinda had acquired a cat, Tiger, who lived with us inside and with whom I shared my living space for thirteen years. I made no attempt to engage with Tiger, learn about her, or even learn about her species. Looking back now, I probably thought there was nothing to learn. Luckily for all of us, especially Oscar, Catherine is a voracious reader and frequently went to our local library for both pleasure reading and information. Within days of Oscar's arrival, she brought home about a half dozen books about cats and how to care for them.

Since Oscar entered my life, I have read numerous books about cats, cat care, cat feeding and animal communication. Some books were better than others, but all had at least a few bits and pieces of useful information. In the first batch that Catherine brought home, we hit the jackpot. Over the following weeks, I learned so much about Oscar and his species that I felt as though a whole new world had opened to me

Probably the single most useful piece of information we learned in that first exposure was that cats are much more social than we had ever known or believed. As a "dog" person, I had assumed that cats were aloof, indifferent, and uncaring about people, other cats and anything other than their next meal. In fact, while cats are solitary hunters (it does not take a pack to hunt a mouse) and want to have claim to a hunting territory, in their "off" hours, when they're not earning their living as hunters, many cats seem to enjoy being with others of their kind. As with humans, there is a broad spectrum of desire for interaction with others. Cats who do not have to hunt, and neutered males who do not have to compete for breeding privileges, are, in most cases, quite social and friendly. This is also true of most cats who are socialized with humans during their first seven to twelve weeks of life.

Another extremely critical lesson we learned during that time was about the feeding of cats. Cats are what is known as obligate carnivores, which means they need to have a meat diet. Omnivores can survive on both plant and meat protein, but cats, to be healthy and thrive, need to have meat. There are specific enzymes in meat that are essential for a cat's nutrition, so instead of meat and potatoes, it's skip the potatoes and serve only the meat. Moisture or hydration, which is to say water, is another big issue for cats. Most cat scholars agree the species originated in the deserts of northern Africa. These cats, living in such an arid environment, had to get most of their water from the prey they captured and ate. Today's domestic house cats have evolved with an inadequate thirst mechanism. Most cats who eat only dry food, or kibble as it's known, are in a state of constant subclinical dehydration.

While Catherine and I were busy learning about cats from books, Oscar was busy learning about us from experience. We had no idea where he had been prior to his being found wandering the school grounds, but he seemed quite at home with us humans and showed no indication that he had been a feral or wild cat. He showed no inclination to bolt out the door, used his litter box when he needed it, and gave all signs that he was a happy, contented, domesticated cat.

At the same time, we humans had much to discover about our new family member. He was filled with an energetic life-force unlike any other we had ever experienced. Our first days and months together were exploration periods for all of us. As Oscar raided the cupboard, tore through boxes of pasta and bags of energy bars, we came to understand that his behavior was not due to hunger but, rather, to sheer curiosity and a cautionary need to know his territory. Cats are predators, but they are also prey. Through thousands of years of evolution, they have had to learn to be extremely careful and be aware of everything around them. Every open closet, drawer, or cabinet (and many which he learned to open), became a new adventure for Oscar to check out. We found that baby locks on drawers and cabinets worked quite well in keeping our food stores intact, and once Oscar learned where he could go and where he could not, things were much calmer around the house.

Oscar proved himself to be quite a social being. He actively sought to engage with us in various forms of play including toys and such games as hide-and-seek. He would engage us in the latter by going someplace, mostly out of sight (he frequently forgot about his tail), then meowing for us to come find him. The fact that he wanted to engage with us, and knew how to actively get us to play with him, was amazing to me. We also observed his fabulous athletic prowess. He was more agile than any human athlete, capable of leaping over furniture in a single bound, twisting in mid-air, and having an uncanny ability to judge space and distance, so that he always landed perfectly.

When Oscar turned about eight months old, we realized his life would be enriched with a companion cat. When we traveled, we had a cat/house sitter who stayed at the house. Living with someone who had to go off to work, however, left him with much more time all alone than living with two retired people who were home most of the day. Plus, just as we benefit from human interaction, many cats also benefit from socialization with their own species.

With this in mind, we went to one of Rescue House's quarterly adoption fairs. There we met "Jack", a black cat with luminescent green eyes, who had been found as a very young kitten along the roadside. He was too young to have been properly weaned from his mother and required bottle-feeding and lots of human contact. His growth had been stunted, and he had been undernourished but, after several months of care at Rescue House, he was looking much better. At the time, I was uncertain as to whether we were destined for one another, but I could not help but focus on Jack. A lot of our friends at the adoption fair urged us to adopt Jack, and I was certainly drawn to him.

It took a few days to complete the process, but soon this delicate soul came to our home. After careful consideration, we decided to name him Oliver, after Oliver Twist, the title character of the famous novel by Charles Dickens. It's the story of a young street orphan in nineteenth century London who finally finds a home of love and acceptance. The name seemed very appropriate for our little orphan.

Not only was Oliver physically underdeveloped, he also required behavioral modification. Having been separated too early from his mother and littermates, he hadn't fully learned "cat manners". With a tendency to nip and nibble on our fingers, he had to learn the ways of his new universe. Slowly, but surely, with our help and that of his feline brother, he adjusted.

OLIVER

Socializing the two was a step into the unknown. At the time, neither Catherine nor I fully understood how to optimize the introduction process. We just introduced five-month-old Oliver into Oscar's established territory, without paying heed to the preliminaries. We humans would probably react negatively if a stranger was shoved into our home, and we were told we were going to be roommates. It is the same way with cats, who are, after all very territorial beings. Ideally, as we know now, when a new cat is introduced into a home several steps of preliminary introduction should happen before the cats meet face-to-face. For starters, a scent exchange is done with a blanket or dry washcloth before the new cat even enters the home. Scent is a primary means of identification and communication for cats, and this way the cats get to "meet" each other before they actually come face to face. Then the new animal is isolated in a separate space so he can adapt to his new environment a little at a time. This is done so the first cat does not feel his entire space has been invaded. Next, feeding takes place on opposite sides of a closed door so each can have a positive experience while in close proximity of the other. After a period of time (variable, but usually one to ten days depending on the players), the cats can meet each other. Since we were oblivious to these guidelines, Catherine and I allowed Oliver to roam freely from the first day, and the two cats bonded very quickly. I can only attribute this swift bonding period to the youthful age of both cats, and Oscar's joyful approach to life.

Almost immediately, the two became as brothers. Feline romping and wrestling became a way of life in our home; and incredibly, the two took turns playing with toys, each yielding to the other and playing at intervals. Oscar would step to one side, without any squabbles or incidents, almost inviting Oliver to take his place. Virtually everything was shared, including food, toys and affection time. Food is sometimes an issue in multiple animal homes, but we had open grazing with food always available. There was never an issue of which bowl to eat from, when to eat, or even problems with overeating.

All the while, we humans looked on in delight and amazement. Never would I have believed that "taking turns" and sharing would be within cats' psychological and emotional makeup. There they were, two divine creatures in our midst, teaching us life lessons about emotional intelligence, bonding, and empathic intuitiveness. No longer did I feel that they were simply instinctual beings, incapable of formulating thoughts. Soon, I began to sense that if I only learned to listen, there would be further untapped insights yet to unfold.

CHAPTER 8

THE OBE JUAN PHENOMENON

Oscar and Oliver continued to bond and, though not litter mates, grew closer by the day. We were becoming a very tightly knit family. However, while the felines of our group were territorial and quite content to stay in one place, Catherine and I still had the urge to travel and see new places and meet new people. This presented a problem, but as with all things in Divine Order, it was resolved with a win–win resolution.

The solution to the problem began to unfold when Catherine and I attended a family wedding and found ourselves seated next to my once-removed cousin, Ernie. Growing up, my closest family playmates were my cousins, Brenda, Bonnie and Rick, all within a few years in age of my brother Bob and me. Ernie was one of Cousin Bonnie's children and was the same age as my eldest daughter, Trace. His mother, Bonnie, had passed away, but my other cousins had moved to San Diego many years before. After his mother died, Ernie also decided to head west.

So, there we were at the wedding of Cousin Rick's daughter Erica when Ernie and I had the opportunity to become re-acquainted. I did not know Ernie well, but as we talked, I learned a lot about him. As it turned out, he had just been laid off from his job as an illustrator and was making ends meet by renting a room from a friend. During our conversation, I learned that Ernie liked cats and I immediately asked whether he would be willing to stay with our boys when we traveled. Ernie readily agreed, and so began his new life as a part time cat-sitter – to the tremendous relief of Catherine and me, and the even greater delight of Oscar and Oliver. Shortly after that, he found work and started a new career, but over the years has continued to stay with the boys when we go on our various trips.

When we weren't traveling, Catherine and I continued to visit regularly at The Rescue House adoption fairs to help out with the orphaned cats. In one memorable instance, I held a twelve-year-old cat on my lap for about a half hour. Laddie was a white-coated beauty who exuded very low energy and was clearly out of sorts. I later learned that his elderly person had passed away, and her children had taken Laddie and his housemate, Murphy, to a veterinarian to have them euthanized. Fortunately, their vet knew about Rescue House and moved these sweet souls into the system for adoption. It is the policy of the Rescue House to keep bonded pairs of cats together, but there was a mix-up and Laddie was left by himself. While Laddie was sent back to the vet to have a benign cyst removed from his neck, Murphy was adopted. I could sense Laddie's loneliness and sadness at losing his person and being separated from his friend. But even then, I could also feel a calmness and presence about him that indicated he was not panicked by the situation, and would roll with the punches.

Clearly, something had to be done about this dear, lovely being. After spending time sitting with him, I felt very drawn to helping him. We felt our cat family was complete, so Catherine and I spent the next six months attempting to find a suitable home for him, questioning everyone from our real estate agent to my mother-in-law. Finally, we decided to foster Laddie and provide a home environment for him while he waited for the quarterly adoption fairs.

The only remaining question was, how would Oscar and Oliver react to the presence of another cat in their midst? To find out their thoughts on the matter, Joan Star, the co-founder of Rescue House, suggested that we contact Dr. Jeri Ryan, a nationally known professional animal communicator. At first, I did not believe that such a thing was possible. After all, they were just cats. How could they have thoughts about something like this? To say I was skeptical would have been a gross understatement. I did not see how such communication could take place, but when Rescue House offered to pay for the session, I consented and resolved to keep an open mind.

At the time, Catherine and I knew nothing about animal communication. We could not fathom the nature of such a conversation or even how it was possible. Dr. Ryan, however, was genuine and expert and put us instantly at ease. She lived in San Francisco and had no physical contact with us or the cats, but she assured us that she would use intuitive communication to connect with them, and hold a conversation with each of them. She would write down the conversation, word for word, then call us and relay the "chat" to us. This seemed like really far out, "airy-fairy" stuff to me, but in my twenty-eight years in the Navy, I had come to understand that, sometimes, one needs to just button one's lip, listen and learn. The results of this encounter absolutely blew me away and altered my life.

After communicating with the boys, Jeri reported that both were empathetic to Laddie's plight, and they agreed to the have him come to live with us in foster care. Although the outcome of the conversations was meaningful, even more startling and significant was my realization that Jeri had been in communication with our two cats, sight unseen, over a distance of five hundred miles. She described the personalities of each cat precisely, the way they lived their lives, what they did, and what each liked and disliked. She left absolutely no doubt in my mind that she was "talking" to Oscar and Oliver. The thoughts she relayed from each boy were in complete alignment with the way their personalities manifested.

So foster care it was. Before Laddie's arrival to our home, we first did a scent exchange with all of the cats. We took a blanket which Oscar and Oliver had both slept on to Laddie's current foster home so he could become accustomed to their scents. Then we rubbed a dry washcloth on Laddie and brought it to our house so the two boys could smell him. When he arrived at our house, we initially set up him up in Catherine's office by himself. He had a day or so to get used to us and his new environment so he could feel safe. Then, while Oscar and Oliver napped in my office, we would close that door and allow our new family member to freely explore the house. Somewhat slow-moving and cautious at first, he tentatively checked out all of the spaces and began to look quite comfortable. He soon began to "play paws" under the door of his room with his housemates, until eventually we opened the door, and the three began to share their turf.

After only a few weeks, we realized that he had chosen us as his people, and we rapidly dispelled all ideas of ever giving him up. So Laddie started his new life with us, complete with a new name. He dutifully wrote to the Rescue House, via one of his staffers (read: yours truly). To be sure, I was a grateful conduit. I offer the e-mail correspondence here, by way of introduction to the cat who would come to be called "John Obediah" (a/k/a "Obe Juan"):

Sent: Tuesday, July 20, 2010 11:13 a.m.

Subject: John Obediah

To My Rescue House Friends,

I have asked a staff member to write this on a computer, since few of you speak cat, and I don't see the need to learn such a primitive method of communicating as e-mail. There have been several changes in my life about which I would like to inform you. First is a name change. Laddie was a good name when I was a strapping young cat, but for the distinguished gentleman I have become, not so much. I have, therefore, changed my name to "John Obediah". John is a European/biblical name, meaning "God is gracious". Obediah is a Hebrew name, meaning "messenger of God". I certainly see myself as a messenger of Divine Graciousness; so, it is a most fitting name. I have decided to make a few alterations to make the name more worldly. Americans like to shorten long names into nicknames. I like the idea of a Spanish flavor to my name; and in Asia, the family name is generally used first. So, having combined all of these ideas, my friends can now call me "Obe Juan."

Next, I regret to inform you that I no longer require the services of the Rescue House. You have all been wonderful to me during my temporary time of indisposition, but I find that I must answer to a higher calling, and it is time to move on. In that vein, I find my accommodations in this new place to be acceptable, and my new friends, Oscar and Oliver, have asked me to stay on and help them with their life-long project of training the staff here. I must go where I am most needed. I will have my people contact your people to see about setting this up as to paperwork and finances.

I want to express my heartfelt appreciation to all of the staff at Rescue House, not just for the love, care, and affection bestowed on me, but also for all of the great things you do for all of my "peeps" who have been with you or are awaiting new homes. You are earning much merit and building good karma in Pussycat Paradise. Keep doing what you are doing, and if you are fortunate, you might just be able to earn enough to come back as a cat in your next life.

You have been the purr-fect place for me to be in my time of great need. I will always remember you with great fondness. Please feel free to come by and visit anytime. I would love to see you.

Peace and blessings, Obe Juan (by staffer Gerald)

P.S. I forgot to mention that my health is great. These two young whippersnapper cats have me running, jumping, and playing, and I feel five years younger.

I tried my best to convey accurately what I thought may be Obe Juan's feelings and intentions. I was new to the realm of feline sentience/communication, and I wanted to do justice to our new arrival and add a little humor to the process.

Despite the pre-arrival intuitive communication, the integration was not entirely problem-free. While Oscar showed non-aggressive interest in the new kid on the block, Oliver challenged him with stare-downs, designed to scare him off. It was as if Oliver had learned the techniques of Sun Tzu's *The Art of War*[iii] in which Sun Tzu discusses the advantages of posturing, maneuvering and outsmarting the enemy without physical fighting.

Perhaps it was the other way around and Sun Tzu had learned from observing animals. After all, in the wild, same species animals seldom fight to the death or even inflict serious injury. I have seen numerous nature films where same species animals will posture and sometimes fight, usually over territory or breeding rights. Seldom is the in-fighting lethal whereas a different species trying to attack or prey on that group might suffer an injury or even death.

To return to the realm of our cats, what happened next was nothing less than extraordinary. On three separate occasions, Catherine and I observed Oscar as he watched Oliver and Obe Juan engage in a stare-down across the room from each other. On each occasion, Oscar got up from where he was and moved to position himself exactly half way between them at a ninety-degree angle to "the stare". Oscar stared off into space for a minute, turned his head to look at one of them, and then turned his head to look at the other, and then looked back into space. He was clearly acting as a peacemaker. I could almost hear him say, "Okay guys, we're all family here. Let's stay calm, be nice to each other and lose the attitude." This method of conflict resolution, employed several times, dissipated the tension — but only for a while.

One morning, while I was relaxing with a book, I looked up and noticed that the stack of newspapers to be recycled had been disrupted. Upon closer inspection, I discovered cat feces on the papers. As we cleaned up, Catherine and I also observed the presence of waste matter on the mail on our dining room table - a place where cats were not allowed. We left the room to dispose of the mess and came back forty-five seconds later to find cat poop on the table itself. As we stood near the table in disbelief, three pairs of cat eyes looked up at us with what seemed to be complete innocence and curiosity.

Baffled, but suspecting Oliver to be the cause, I called Jeri Ryan, who promised to speak with the boys and get back to us later that evening. Jeri reiterated her approach: to convey the animals' feelings and emotions through their eyes, take notes, and then relay the conversation to us. When we reconvened over the phone that night, she reported the following conversation with Oliver.

Jeri: "Oliver, we have a problem. Can you help us? Someone is pooping outside of the litter box. Could it be you?"
Oliver (after a long pause): "Yes."
Jeri: "There must be a reason. Can you tell me what it is?"
Oliver: "They changed everything, made everything different."
Jeri: "How have things changed?"
Oliver: (feeling frustrated and upset): "It's the other cat. I've lost my best friend."
Jeri: "Do you mean Oscar?"
Oliver: "Yes."
Jeri: "Why do you think that you have lost your best friend?"
Oliver: "Because Oscar and the other cat are together all the time."
Jeri: "Have you spoken to Oscar about this?"
Oliver: "No."
Jeri: "Why not?"
Oliver: "I'm too shy."
Jeri: "I think that you should speak to Oscar about how you feel. This behavior is not good, and you have to tell Oscar what you just told me."

Jeri went on to explain to Oliver that not using the litter box was extremely upsetting to us and that she would communicate his frustrations to us so he would not have to do that anymore. Since that time, there has never been another "outside the litter box" issue with Oliver or any of the boys.

Jeri also asked Oliver for his help with Obe Juan. She told him about Obe Juan losing his person and his housemate and asked if he would help Obe by being his friend. She asked if he would show him around, helping him when he needed it, and let him know that he was loved.

One other part of Jeri's conversation with Oliver was to give him a job in the family. She explained to us that it useful to give animals specific duties in the household to let them know they belong, they are important, and they are needed. Oliver's job was to help find insects, mice and spiders in our house. We knew he took his new job seriously when for the next two nights we were awakened in the night by his meowing and calling to us. When Catherine went to see what the hub-bub was about, there was Oliver, crouching over a tiny little insect in the carpet, letting us know he was on the job!

Then, Jeri spoke with Oscar and Obe Juan. Oscar seemed fine, but Obe Juan was grieving and depressed about the loss of his former person and of his cat friend Murphy. He expressed gratitude to us for taking him in and giving him a home and was genuinely happy to be with us, but he still missed his other life very much.

While this communication solved the litter box issue and started the boys on their way to developing a strong bond, it had an even more profound effect on me. With Oscar's arrival in my life, I experienced a dawning of awareness that animals had thoughts, feelings, and emotions. I could not look into their sparkling eyes and not perceive intelligence and a sense of self. Now, I understood that animals can communicate those feelings to us humans — if we only learn to listen to them.

After Jeri's intervention, the bonding process between all three cats continued to develop, and Oliver felt that he was truly part of a friendship circle – like the Three Musketeers.

Suddenly, he realized that he had not only one best friend, but two! His world was completely changing, as was mine.

An entire universe of possibilities began to open up and gently engulf me. Jeri said the ability to communicate with animals is not a unique "gift". Rather, it is part of the process of all life, and every human possesses it. In fact, we are born with it. We begin to suppress it when we learn spoken language, but it is still there for all of us, all the time.

That part of me which studied science and engineering for all of those years, then used this knowledge to fly Navy jets from aircraft carriers and jumbo jets across the ocean, wanted to deny this and say that it could not be. After all, we lived in a scientific world, ruled by laws of physics. But there before me was the proof of what the three amigos were doing, and more significantly, deep inside, my Divine Guidance was telling me, *This is real!*

OBE JUAN AND OLIVER THE DAY
AFTER TALKING TO JERI RYAN

CHAPTER 9

A LEAP OF FAITH

My inner guidance may have been saying of intuitive communication, *This is real*, but my outer self, trained as an engineer, was objecting. It was difficult to go from being a left-brained empiricist, seemingly hardwired for strict discipline, science-based subject matter and detail, to being a right-brained intuitive. It seemed I had too many years of thinking and being one way to switch suddenly to an entirely new outlook.

I had enlisted in the Navy as a means of escaping home and "seeing the world". After initial training at boot camp, I was assigned to a small ship in Norfolk, Virginia, where I learned there was little joy in swabbing decks and washing dishes. My Executive Officer, or second in command, recommended I apply for an appointment to the Naval Academy. There I could get a college education and become an officer. I quickly did so, was accepted, and was soon off to one of the finest engineering schools in the country.

The Naval Academy is a fully accredited four-year engineering school. Students, called midshipmen, study classical science, engineering, math, physics, and chemistry, as well as more specialized topics, such as navigation, weapons systems, and leadership. As a military school, discipline is strict, attention to detail is fanatic, and thinking "outside the box" is not encouraged.

Upon graduating from the Naval Academy and going to flight school, I was immediately deployed to Vietnam, where I eventually accrued more than four hundred hours of combat flying. When I returned from Vietnam, I was assigned to the Naval Post-Graduate School in Monterey, California, to pursue a Master's degree in Aeronautical Engineering.

My post-graduate studies (a two-year intensive curriculum of math and science) came to an abrupt halt after one year, due to my alcoholism. By this time, I was so steeped in postulates, theorems, and 'proven' causation, that if an idea or theory was not grounded in science, it simply did not exist within my realm of understanding. So while I had heard of such esoteric concepts as mental telepathy and psychic ability, I relegated them to the categories of pseudo-science, connivance and/or delusion. Such ideas were in direct conflict with my idea of the knowable universe and were completely contrary to what I considered to be the 'educated' view of the how the world works.

My view had begun to change through the process of recovery (as part of AA's 12-Step Program) and profound religious and spiritual contemplation. I had come to realize that while we are all distinct individuals, each with our own capabilities, we are also, *all of us*, connected, as one, to and through Divine Intelligence. All of these spiritual ideas and my notion of soul-unification through a higher power were confined to the human plane alone.

Then Oscar came along and my perspective changed even more. That first weekend when we did not even consider that he would become a family member, it was quite evident he was a sentient, intelligent being. When he looked at us with awareness, comprehension, and a sense of connection, I knew there was a consciousness behind those beautiful golden eyes. After we had realized that he would become part of our lives, it was necessary to make decisions as to how this intelligent, loving being would fit into our human world.

Catherine and I mutually agreed that Oscar would be an indoor cat. We did not want him to be exposed to the risks of predation, traffic, or communicable diseases. Outdoor cats typically have an average lifespan of three to five years compared to that of well-fed, well-cared-for indoor cats who, on average, enjoy eighteen to twenty years on earth. Cats are genetically predisposed to roam and hunt. In their dual prey/predator roles, staking out and observing changes in their territories are high on their list of survival skills. However, "roaming" is synonymous with "patrolling" a given territory, which is usually not very large. Patrolling a house, for example, meets the instinctual needs of indoor cats, who are quite content to do a daily patrol.

Oscar, in keeping with his innate love of the outdoors, frequently sits near windows and observes activity in the outside world. The living room of our townhouse has a large picture window that almost reaches to the floor, giving him a view of the canyon behind our home, which often captivates him for many hours.

One evening at dusk, about six months after he came to live with us, Catherine and I were in an adjacent room watching TV when Oscar came streaking to the doorway of the room and came to an immediate halt. For a moment, he looked at us with wide eyes and a trembling body, then flew back into the living room. A few seconds later, he repeated that behavior, barely coming into the room, looking at us with the same wide, excited eyes, then returning to the window. The message could not have been clearer, even for those not versed in animal communication: "People, you gotta come see this!" So, into the living room we went. Looking through the window, we spotted a coyote walking on the verge of the canyon just ten or twelve feet from the window. This was a fairly routine occurance and not an unusual sight for us. We live on the edge of a large wilderness park and there are many coyotes in the area. It was one of the main reasons that Oscar was an indoor cat. However, for him, it was a new sighting, and he felt compelled to warn us of the danger. He didn't run and hide, or simply stay there and observe - he came to warn his family. I realized then that not only was he sentient and intelligent, but he was also a being with emotions, loyalties, and a desire and need to communicate.

As for Oliver, he is an entirely different entity; with his very own set of traits and characteristics, and a personality (or, perhaps, *felinality*) all his own. He is much more timid than Oscar, yet much more vocal. Where Oscar may want to be the center of attention, Oliver is quite happy to take a quiet nap under the bed.

Observing the two interact, learn to share toys and territory, and bond with one another was truly a revelation. It became very obvious to me these were not just "dumb animals" operating on instinct. They are thoughtful, caring souls who thoroughly enjoy life – all while liking each other and us humans.

Further epiphanies surfaced when Obe Juan entered our lives and, with him, Jeri Ryan, who introduced us to animal communication. Jeri told us that intuitive animal communication is a capability that all of us have. It is a skill that can be learned and developed by virtually anyone through willingness, an open heart, and practice. Even as she was telling us this, I wondered *Is she just saying that because she can do it, or is it truly possible that anyone can learn animal communication, even me?* As I began to research the topic, I soon discovered that animal communication is like learning any foreign language. For example, if you want to learn Spanish you have to read books, study, and gradually become familiar with the syntax, grammar, and sentence formation. If you work at it and practice, practice, practice, you will eventually be able to state, "*Hablo español.*"

Being an engineer, my first inclination was to delve into this topic from the basis of research. So, my first order of business was a trip to the library to seek out books on this new and, to me, untapped world of animal communication. Although psychic and telepathic communication has been studied for a number of years, little exploration had been done in the field of intuitive animal communication until J. Allen Boone wrote *Kinship With All Life*[iv] first released in 1954. The book celebrated the author's relationship with Strongheart, a German Shepherd movie star. As his caretaker, Boone quickly became aware of Strongheart's intelligence and bonding capacity. This prompted Boone to delve more deeply into the idea of actual communication between species. Over the course of time, he discovered that Strongheart had thoughts, emotions, and feelings, and if he (Boone) learned to pay attention, the two of them could have actual two-way communication.

Extending this idea to other species, Boone realized that all beings are perceptive, feeling, thinking creatures. He even devoted a portion of his book to his conversations with Freddie the fly. Prior to hearing Dr. Jeri Ryan's communication with our cats, I would not have even considered picking up Boone's book. As I continued to read more than a dozen books on the topic, I began to realize intuitive animal communication is, in fact, very real. I further started to realize that I, too, could learn to engage in such communication.

No doubt, throughout history, individuals such as Saint Francis of Assisi (1181-1226) had the ability to communicate inter-species. He was always depicted in the company of animals, who purportedly listened to his sermons and followed his bidding. Unfortunately, we have no way of knowing if he was engaging in actual two-way communication, as he did not record his thoughts on the matter. Most likely, he could not write or talk about it without fear of chastisement — or even worse.

According to Christian church doctrine, animals were put on earth to serve mankind. The Bible tells us that man has dominion over all animals. Although I grew up as a Christian fundamentalist and studied the Bible (dare I say religiously), I have since come to realize the limitations of that way of thinking. The Bible is the religious text of a minority of the world's population, written thousands of years ago by men (without female input). It has been highly edited and translated numerous times. I have come to believe that while the Bible holds much deep wisdom and spiritual truth, the literal interpretation of the text fosters a narrow perspective.

The line of reasoning that postulates one species or one race is better, or should have dominion over another, can be and has been taken one step further, leading to the practice of human servitude and slavery. Throughout much of human history, some people have been subjugated on the basis of racial or gender differentiation. Such dehumanization and belittlement run counter to the awareness that we are all equal, integral parts of the experience of the "All" – that is, the wholeness of which we are all individual components.

In astonishing measure, much of humanity has come to acknowledge that all humans are, or should be, equal. Virtually no country in the modern world legalizes slavery. However, as recently as one hundred fifty-five years ago in the United States, such was not the case. At that time, human subjugation was legal and institutionalized by the government. To a degree, servitude still exists in various forms (including forced child labor, human rights violations against women, sexual slavery, and other crimes against humanity). Judging by reactions in the media, most people are vehemently opposed to all of these forms of servitude. Considering how far we have advanced in a relatively brief time period, it seems natural to envision a point in our future when we will, at last, come to understand that *all* life, irrespective of species, has equal value.

As I read and studied about intuitive animal communication, my scientifically trained engineer's mind continued to battle with my desire to learn this process. I began to realize that understanding the idea of all-life-interconnectedness was (for me, at least) going to take a leap of faith. I can never use the term leap of faith without thinking of a poem by Christopher Logue (frequently attributed to Guillaume Apollinaire), called "Come to the Edge".

Come to the edge
We might fall
Come to the edge
It's too high!
COME TO THE EDGE!
And they came
And he pushed them
And they flew.

For me, the message in that verse is that you never really know what you can achieve until you take that leap of faith, spread your wings, and fly.

My task in "coming to the edge" involved quieting my left-brained logic and reasoning and opening the door to my spirit. I needed to learn how to let other life forms in — beings who, I have learned, are as alive to the processes and ways of the universe as you and I.

One of the most useful writings which helped me to access the more intuitive aspect of myself was Amelia Kinkade's second book, *The Language of Miracles*[v]. Written with the mentorship of Apollo astronaut, Edgar Mitchell, Ph.D. with a foreword by Bernie Siegel, M.D., the book was just what my left-brained, aeronautical engineer's mind needed. It supplied a cogent, scientifically based explanation of how interspecies communication is the transmission of thought-energy at the zero-point energy level of the quantum field. There it was: that term quantum field, an actual scientific concept being applied to what I had been thinking of as more like voodoo magic. It was the beginning of a revelation for me.

This book, like all the others I had read, stressed that we are all born with the ability to communicate with animals. It was all within my grasp. *I can do this!* I thought. Like everyone else, I was born with the ability. I just have to tap into it. The next step was finding a means of learning and just doing it. *Could it be that simple?*

Soon thereafter my daughter, Trace, called and told me about a pet store in the area where four professional animal communicators were scheduled to appear and speak about their work. Eager to begin a new phase in my life, I signed up for the seminar. I had no idea where it all might lead, or what might be the end result. I did know that Oscar had brought me to the edge, and now it was time to take that leap of faith.

CHAPTER 10

EXPLORING THE WILDERNESS OF THE QUANTUM FIELD

As I continued to study this idea of animal communication, one theme consistently surfaced: intuitive communication is part of who and what we universe-dwellers are. All of us are born with that capacity, and each one of us can do it.

As we learn spoken language, we stop using intuitive communication and allow it to slide back into the recesses of our brain where, for most humans, it lies dormant. However, the ability is always there and can be revived at any time. In reality, all of us consistently experience intuitive communication with the animals in our lives, but it is usually a one-way street.

I once communicated with a dog named George who was "acting out" by chewing all sorts of things in the house when his person Susan left to go to work. George was bored, frustrated and a little panicked not knowing if or when Susan was coming back. I'll never forget his reply when I asked him about his frustration. He said "Susan talks to me all the time, but she doesn't understand what I tell her."

Animals pick up on our thoughts, but we are not generally as in tune with theirs. In her book, *The Animal Connection: a Guide to Intuitive Communication with Your Pet*[vi], Judy Meyer explains this process. This book, one of my favorite writings on the topic, is offered in layman's terms and can be read in just over an hour.

At the other end of the spectrum is Amelia Kinkade's work, *The Language of Miracles*, written in collaboration with former astronaut Edgar Mitchell, Ph.D. and noted in the previous chapter. This is a great one for my engineer's left-brained sensibilities, as it explains and demystifies the concept of the quantum energy field. It also explains the zero-point energy of the quantum field and the "how to" of reaching that energy level. Attaining, or at least approaching, the zero-point energy level, must be achieved in order to engage in animal communication. It is in that space that thought-energy is exchanged and interpreted by each intelligent being. For more on this topic, see *Appendix A* of this book.

Initially, the concept of zero-point energy was exceptionally deep and sci-fi-like to me. However, Amelia stresses it is not necessary to know or understand the scientific concepts to talk with animals. So for me, the realization that there *is* a scientific basis, whether I fully understand it or not, takes the whole topic out of the realm of "airy-fairy, booga-booga" magic, and into the zone of scientifically explainable phenomena.

Animal communicators use what is commonly called telepathy to connect with other species. According to Merriam-Webster's dictionary, "telepathy" is defined as "communication from one mind to another by extrasensory means". There is no fairy dust here. Simply expressed, the word "extrasensory" signifies that which is non-local and outside the awareness of our five senses.

It is interesting to note that, in animal communicators' parlance, the word "telepathy" is seldom used, given its tendency to call to mind charlatans and quacks. At the turn of the 19th century, some performers used the term for stage shows and displays of "supernatural" powers. These days most communicators use the expressions "animal communication" and "intuitive animal communication" interchangeably, so as to avoid any negative connotations.

Modern physicists postulate that all of us exist as individual quanta of energy in an infinite field of quantum energy. When we (or any intelligent being) generates a thought, that thought has provable, measurable electrical energy. This thought energy is available and accessible at the zero-point energy of the quantum field, the point at which all life is interconnected. When we lower our individual energy, through stilling our minds, to reach or approach the zero-point energy of the entire field, we can access or "read" the thought energy of other beings. What has been traditionally called "telepathy" is the transference of thought-energy at the zero-point energy of the quantum field.

Because the science of telepathy is not common knowledge among most people, for many it seems we are dealing with the intangible. Skepticism is a natural result and therefore, people tend to "blow off" the idea. Humans want to deal with the "knowable" world of our five physical senses. Consider, however, how in our modern day and age we have expanded the reach of these five senses. We are no longer restricted to idea of communication with members of our tribe who we can hear, or touch, or see. We have moved far beyond that short range with such "magical" ways to communicate as radio, television, the internet, and the now ubiquitous cell phone.

It is, therefore, for me at least, not much of a stretch to consider the possibility of using the intuitive capability with which all of us are born to further increase our ability to communicate. That intuitive capability is always there, we just don't need it or use it to connect with our own species. As our race becomes more aware of the intelligence of the other species with whom we live, we can all open up a whole new world of connecting with them. With practice, much like one learns any new language, one gradually begins to acquire the skill and confidence to be successful.

Communication is an integral, vital part of our everyday experience. When we speak with other humans, we initially formulate thoughts in our brain which are then converted to images or concepts. We then use the tool of language to describe those ideas to our fellow humans. The recipient of the words we speak then decodes the language into concepts or images for his/her brain which completes the cycle. Words can be extremely useful in channeling our ideas into an understandable, recognizable framework, designed to foster mutual understanding. However, not all sentient, intelligent beings require words to accomplish that objective.

Spoken language can also cause us a certain measure of distress. For instance, our internal self-talk (which is not spoken out loud but which takes the form of a conversation with ourselves) can cause all manner of problems. All humans engage in self-talk — that constant chatter in our brains that never seems to let up. In our self-talk we evaluate, judge, discuss, and comment on everything that goes on in our lives. This can lead us down paths of self-doubt, fear, uncertainty, and confusion. Self-talk sometimes gives us cognitive indigestion by forcing us to probe, analyze, and second-guess so much so that we effectively curtail our spiritual sense of simply *being* who we are at the moment and experiencing our true Divine essence. Because animals don't burden themselves with such verbiage (at least, not as we know it), they live in the "now". They are not weighed down or distracted by internal dialogue and are, as Eckhart Tolle tells us in *The Power of Now^vii*, "the guardians of being". While our human self-talk is telling us what we should have done in the past, or what we should do in the future, animals are completely involved in what is going on in their lives in the present moment.

In his book *The Untethered Soul^viii*, Michael Springer talks about "the observer", that part of ourselves which allows us to step back and "watch" our internal dialogue, or self-talk. Being aware that in our true essence we are "the observer", is what allows us to quiet the self-talk of the mind. It is when we quiet that self-talk, a state which many refer to as meditation, that we can approach the zero-point energy of the quantum field.

With practice, returning to our true essence becomes second nature and helps nurture our ability to communicate with other species. When we come alive to the realization of the intelligence of all animate beings and make the effort, we can then begin the process of learning how to listen. By quieting our internal dialogue and calming our minds, we can begin to hear what those species have to say. It's that simple — and that difficult.

Eager to learn the art of intuitive animal communication, Catherine and I decided to attend the seminar that Trace had told us about at a nearby pet store. There were four animal communicators on hand who each gave a fifteen-minute presentation of their knowledge, understanding and methodologies. All of them stated they would go into a meditative-type state and quiet their internal dialogue. They would then envision the energy of the universe flowing from the cosmos, through their heads and into their hearts, or earth's energy flowing from its core through their feet and into their hearts. From that epicenter (the heart), they sent out a beam of energy to the heart of the animal and posed specific questions.

Each of the communicators said the communication happens instantaneously, faster than the speed of light. Typically an answer surfaces before the question is completely asked. Usually, the first thought that comes to mind is the animal answering the question. Receiving answers can be tricky since the animals' responses don't always match our word-centered paradigm. Also, the answers come to us sounding like our self-talk. For example, when asking an animal "Where is your favorite place to sleep?" one might immediately have the thought "In my bed, in the closet", but that "sounds" like one's own internal voice. How, then, can we be sure that we're not making things up? Of course, the best way is to ask for verification from the animal's human guardian. Just pose the same question: "Where does Max like to sleep?" All of the communicators assured us that through repetition and verification the process becomes more natural and slightly easier.

After the communicators at the seminar had given their presentations, there was a question-and-answer period, followed by a short break. During that interval, we could sign up for 'mini' sessions with any or all of the communicators, who would speak with our animals. Catherine and I decided to sign up for two sessions, just to see what the process was like and how accurate it might be.

The results were fascinating. The two women with whom we signed up did not know us or any of our cats, yet they completely nailed each cat's felinality, habits, likes, and dislikes.

Coming on the heels of the experience with Jeri Ryan, there was no longer any doubt in my mind about the reality of animal communication.

What did fill me with doubt was whether or not I could do it. Part of that had to do with my gender. I have observed that as a man, I am in a distinct minority in the field of animal communication. All of the communicators with whom I have met, and those whose works I have read (except J. Allen Boone), are women. There have been many books written and discussions held about women being more intuitive than men, or men being more left-brained than women. Current research indicates this is more cultural bias than fact, however, from my experience, animal communication is a field in which, at this time, women far outnumber the men. I believe that as we continue to explore the science of the quantum field, the whole concept of animal communication will move out of the realm of intuition and become widely accepted as hard science.

As I continued to read and learn more about animal communication, I decided to test my abilities. I still had many doubts but, after speaking with several animal communicators and reading extensively on the subject, I found that the same concerns were repeatedly expressed. Virtually everyone who embarked on the journey was faced with self-doubt and the same questions about themselves: *Is it possible for me to do this? Can I talk with animals, and will they understand me? Will I seem like the biggest idiot in the world if I 'talk' to some critter?* Every communicator (including experts) has to overcome that hesitancy and make the leap. As for me - well, there was only one way to find out if I could to it, and being somewhat adventurous, I decided to try.

I live in the southwest part of the country, on the edge of a large 5,200-acre regional park with undeveloped canyon land

and miles of hiking trails. One of the many trailheads is only about a two-hundred-yard walk from our place, and I am a frequent hiker in the park.

On one bright Sunday morning, after one of my many readings on the sentience of animal life, I decided to go hiking. As I was walking along enjoying the moment, I came across a six- to seven-foot-long Western Diamondback rattlesnake, lying across the trail, sunning itself. I stopped short and ventured to communicate intuitively with the sunbather.

"You're so beautiful. I'm so happy to meet you", I began. "It's great that we can be together like this but I am a human, and I have to stay on this path. You are a snake and can go anywhere in the park. Since I have to stay on the trail, I'm going to walk around you so that I can continue my hike. I won't disturb you. You are entirely safe, as am I. We are friends. So, I'm just going to squeeze around the edge here."

Proceeding on my way, I edged in front of the snake so that he could see me, continuing to look at him while readying my hiking poles, in case he rattled or became excited. To my surprise, however, my new friend didn't coil up or budge an inch. He just continued to lie across the trail, soaking up the warmth of the sun. When I reached the other side, I turned back and spoke with him again.

"There's a nice spot behind you up on the bank. This place is not very safe for you. A lot of humans use this trail. Many of them are afraid of snakes, and that triggers their inner response to kill you. So, you can go to the spot behind you, get all of the warmth that you want, and be safe, away from the trail. No one will notice you there. I suggest you do that."

Barely had I finished my communication when the Diamondback turned one hundred eighty degrees and moved off the trail to the very spot that I had mentioned. I was truly stunned. *Had I really just communicated with a snake, and had he responded to me?* Either this was one of the biggest coincidences I had ever experienced, or I had just communicated with another species.

As I noted before, intuitive animal communication does not discriminate as to species. Insects are sentient, intelligent beings and perfectly capable of communication as J. Allen Boone recounted in his book about Strongheart. He told of a long conversation with a fly which he named Freddie. I, too, personally experienced this during one of my hikes. Gnats began to buzz around my face so I decided to see if I could connect with these guys and get some relief from all the attention. I had nothing to lose, so I struck up a conversation with my traveling companions.

"Listen, guys! Here's the deal. I'm a human, and it's very distracting to have gnats buzzing around my ears, nose, and eyes. What's more, I might accidently inhale and kill you, so I have to ask you to go buzz somewhere else. If you need moisture in the form of human perspiration, please go to my arms or my legs; but please, stay away from my face. I don't want you to get hurt."

As with my friend, the snake, there was an almost instant response. The gnats flew away from my face and did not bother me again. They did not even go to my arms or legs but left me alone. I now do this every time I hike (speaking with different gnats each time, I suppose), and the gnats always respect my request and leave me to myself.

On that first occasion, as the gnats flew away, I came to realize three things. First, they were not going after me personally but, rather, just trying to earn their living and feed themselves. It was not an attack on me, Gerald; it was a different species doing what it had to do to survive. The second revelation was that, perhaps, the gnats did not know that I was a sentient being with thoughts and feelings. To them, I merely represented a feeding station, but when I took the time to connect with them and express myself, they were very willing to cooperate. Third, (and perhaps most importantly), we communicated through the medium of Divine Universal Intelligence. We humans believe that we think by using our brains, but gnats do not have brains as we know them, so how can they communicate or be understood? Is it, perhaps, Divine Universal Intelligence, operating through the soup of the quantum field in which all of us exist? Is the Oneness of all life energy the medium for sharing thoughts with other species?

Not too long after my experience with gnats, I went backpacking alone into a wilderness area. At the campground, I set up my tent, and after securing my food in an animal-proof bag (which I placed on the ground), I went to get water. When I returned, I found a squirrel eagerly trying to get into the bag. As I approached, the intruder scurried off. Sensing the creature's frustration, I decided once again to see if I could communicate with another species.

"I understand that you want to get to my food. In fact, I have more than I need and will be happy to leave some for you tomorrow when I pack up. For now, please leave my campsite and don't try to eat my food. I have plenty of nuts, and I will leave you some." Immediately, a thought flashed into my mind: "Why don't you give them to me now, and I won't bother you anymore?"

Wait a minute! Did I just hear what I think I heard? Of course, my internal self-talk immediately took over. *I just made that up! A squirrel can't talk like that! Or can it? Are we communicating?* Returning to the present moment, I took a deep breath, calmed my inner dialogue, and then thought, *what the heck, let's find out.* I reached into the bag and pulled out a supply of peanuts. Spotting the squirrel on a tree branch, fifteen to twenty feet from the campground, I approached, left my offering on a branch near him, and returned to the camp. As I looked back, I observed my new friend gathering up the nuts and dashing off. I did not see him again.

I had to ask myself, *Was that just another coincidence?* Perhaps, but I don't think so. The two of us had engaged in mutually beneficial negotiations. I had become convinced of the reality of animal communication, and I had read that all humans can do it. As I tested my capability in these instances, I was coming to believe that I really could do this. I could not only send thoughts to animals that they could "hear" and understand, but I could also "hear" their responses.

As the enormous reality of these experiences began to sink in, I still had no concept of the vastness of the quantum field, the exchange of thought-energy, or how the whole thing really worked. Luckily for me, however, I did not have to know the details of how it worked. At that point, all I knew was that it *did*, and I wanted to learn more.

CHAPTER 11

THE MYSTERY
OF THE BOAT

In my journey toward a deeper understanding of the oneness and interconnectedness of all life, I have come to believe that all of us are psychic. In fact, that is precisely what each of the many books on animal communication tells us. The little things that we pass off as inconsequential — those soft, nudging whispers that we often ignore — are, in fact, indicators of the existence and inner workings of our intuitive senses.

In her book, *Ask Your Animal*[ix], Marta Williams lists seven common psychic experiences: "(1) knowing when someone is lying to you or manipulating you; (2) getting a strong feeling that you should or shouldn't do something and then finding out that you were right; (3) knowing, from a distance, that something is wrong with your baby or one of your animals; (4) thinking of someone and getting a call or letter from that person; (5) knowing how someone is feeling; (6) knowing that something is going to happen before it does, and (7) knowing who is calling before picking up the phone."

For most of my life before Oscar, these seven indicators of psychic ability, similarly mentioned in every book on the topic of animal communication, were not even in my realm of consciousness. During my lifetime, I had never really paid attention to such events as I have described above. The very few times when these things happened, I assumed they were mere coincidences. Therefore, I questioned how they could be actual signs of my psychic capacity. After all, if it is true that these indicators are proof of psychic ability and I didn't experience them, didn't that mean I don't have "the gift"? Alternatively, is it possible that after a lifetime of black and white analyses and formula-based reasoning, I had deeply suppressed the ability and, therefore, had to take a proverbial "leap of faith" in order to test and develop my skills?

Ultimately, I decided that if I were to explore further this world of animal communication, it would be best for me not to question everything too deeply — at least, not at the beginning. Questions can lead to more and more questions and I realized I could find myself "going down the rabbit hole" in an infinite whirlpool of inquiries, going nowhere. Instead, I resolved just to go along for the ride and see where it all led.

Having already taken an initial "leap" by attending the seminar at our local pet store, Catherine and I went a step further and asked the communicators to conduct individual readings with our 'boys'. One communicator, Lisa Larson, particularly impressed us. When we talked with her by phone, we instantly took a liking to her, and received a "good vibe" — one of those small whispers to which I referred earlier. Was that a psychic experience? Perhaps.

We were so intrigued by Lisa's talents that we asked if we could receive training from her. She didn't have any classes scheduled at the time, so she offered to give us a six-week private course, once a week for an hour and a half. Eagerly, though with slight trepidation (we were, after all, jumping into unknown territory), Catherine and I decided to go ahead with our plan.

This was such unchartered territory for me that I realized I had to adopt an attitude of, *I'm not sure if I really believe this, and I don't know how it works, but I'll give it my best shot and judge by the results.* My self-doubt had come front and center, but as I learned more about animal communication (and even about communication between humans) I realized that doubt is a natural consequence of the process. Even experienced, professional animal communicators must deal with the fact that their communications with other species are not one hundred percent accurate.

In fact, most humans (even when using a common language), rarely achieve completely accurate communication. Frequently, what I say to someone in our common language is not what is heard, and vice versa. I may have a thought that I convey to another person in what I believe to be perfectly understandable terms, but it isn't understood by them in the way I meant it. While the other individual *hears* my words, their personal filters may assign a different meaning to them than what I intend.

As I worked toward my master's degree in Counseling Psychology, one of the class exercises entailed talking with another person and receiving feedback as to what the listener 'heard'. It was incredible how often highly educated people would miss the accuracy mark in a two-way exchange of information. Catherine and I have been married more than thirty years and, at times, we miscommunicate on something as simple as a grocery list. Although we are of the same species, and speak the same native language, discrepancies occasionally arise. So, when two sentient beings of different species communicate in a language not common to both of them, the very same issues can occur.

Animal communication is non-verbal, which means the dialog is taking place in our heads. A problem for us humans is that we also have a constant flow of 'self-talk' going on in our minds. When we communicate with an animal at the quantum level, that animal's responses are perceived as 'sounding' exactly like our own self-talk. Immediately then, self-doubt kicks in, and the question arises: *Was that me, or was it my animal friend who had that thought?* Or, more frequently, for a beginner like me, the question is: *Am I making that up?*

The key is to silence — or at least quiet — one's mental chatter. This was almost impossible for me to do at first. With practice, I slowly began to disregard my self-talk, so as to focus on the animal and the thought-energy being transferred at the zero-point energy of the quantum field.

On our initial day of our training, Lisa led us in a guided meditation. She wanted us to quiet our minds and enter into a meditative state, focusing on our breathing and staying in the here and now. She instructed us to release any random thoughts that came into our awareness and redirect our attention to our breathing. She then showed us pictures of animals featured on her website, and told us to ask a series of questions, for which answers were readily verifiable by the animal's guardian such as: "What is your favorite food?", "Which toy do you like to play with?", "Where do you sleep?", "Are you an indoor or outdoor cat/dog?"

"Write down the first thing that comes into your mind," Lisa advised us. As I later learned, thought energy travels instantaneously in the quantum field — faster than the speed of light. This revelation calls Albert Einstein's (1879-1955) Theory of Relativity into question. Einstein posited that absolutely nothing can travel more quickly than the speed of light, and from this idea, he developed his theory of relativity: E=MC2 (energy equals matter times the speed of light to the second power). Quantum physicists have since discovered that in the quantum energy realm, separate sub-atomic particles can receive and react to information simultaneously, no matter how far apart they may be.

The implication of this revelation is stunning. If Einstein theorized that nothing could travel faster than the speed of light, but quantum physicists have proven that thought-energy has no speed limit and creates instantaneous, simultaneous awareness throughout the field, then the quantum field operates outside the realm of standard Newtonian and Einsteinian physics. It's a whole new ball game — one for which my slide rule (or, these days, my megabyte handheld computer) requires a serious re-calibration.

As we continued our training with Lisa, I felt like a fish out of water. I imposed my own thoughts onto my attempted communications and constantly second-guessed myself. The self-talk and the doubt were resonating in my psyche and making me wonder how it would ever be possible for me to learn how to speak with animals.

Then came my big break-through. Lisa suggested that I speak to her cat Puma, with whom she had lived in Northern California and who had passed away and was now in spirit. She gave me a photo of Puma and asked me to pose questions.

For one of my questions to Puma I asked "What did you like to do in your old home?"

"I liked to sit at the window and watch the boat", came the reply.

What? A boat? Boats and cats are incongruous. *Cats like to sit at windows, but where does the boat come in? Maybe,* I thought, *they lived near a harbor.* My mind wrangled with the issue of what I should record in writing. Having created my own story in my head, I wrote, "I like to sit at the window and look at the boats in the harbor."

When I relayed this to Lisa, she exclaimed, "Wow! That's close! My neighbor was building a boat in her backyard, and Puma used to like to perch on the cat tree, look out of the window, and watch the boat."

I had received the correct input about 'the boat', but the rest of the embellished narrative was my attempt to contextualize what I 'heard' the cat saying. Of course, I had not 'heard' anything. I had a thought in my brain that immediately followed the question I had asked. I did not hear audible words; rather, I had received thought-energy, transferred into and through the quantum field. Most importantly, I had understood Puma's response to the question.

Such were my first baby steps with animal communication. Initially, I was somewhat discouraged at having gotten it 'wrong' about the boats in the harbor, but Lisa seemed very impressed and gave me lots of praise. As I pondered more, I began to realize that I had achieved my goal. I got it! I simply had asked a question and received an answer that my conscious mind would not have provided. In the past, I had had "talks" with the snake, the gnats, and the squirrel, but they were all one way communications with no verification. The results could well have been coincidences. In Lisa's classes, I had experienced some success, but just as many failures. These were simple questions like "What do you like to eat?" or "Where do you like to sleep?" The answers were such that they could have been correct or wrong just by random chance. But to have believed that the boat idea was merely a coincidence would have been quite a stretch. In fact, I had experienced actual and verifiable inter-species communication — maybe at a very elementary level, but certainly, it was a start.

As with learning any new skill or language, one has to practice. Hearing a cat say the word 'boat' to me was a very long way from Jeri Ryan's conversation with Oliver, as he bemoaned losing his best friend Oscar. It was, however, a beginning, and an affirmative indication of what might lie in store if I dedicated myself to learning more.

My positive experience with the mystery of the 'boat' signaled that it was time for me to venture farther and begin talking with other guardians' animal family members. Once again, I was about to be catapulted; but this time, I wasn't on a combat mission. I was about to boldly launch into a realm where I had never before even dreamed of going.

CHAPTER 12

LEARNING IN THE "REAL" WORLD

After finishing our six-week course with Lisa Larson, I was ready to transition into the real world. This brings up the interesting question: exactly what is the "real world?" For most of us the world is that which can be sensed and defined by our five physical senses. Prior to meeting Oscar and becoming his person, I defined the term according to the laws of Newtonian physics. These laws were the basis of my formal education and even after years of spiritual and metaphysical study, I still thought like an engineer. However, with Oscar's arrival to our home, a series of events and learning experiences led me to a new awareness of reality.

Classical physics, a linear method of observing and defining our known universe as we perceive it on a daily basis, has been sharply challenged by non-linear quantum theory. The Newtonian model works well in the world that we see, but with regard to enormous things (such as planets), or infinitesimal things (such as sub- atomic particles), the classical laws break down. This led to what many now call the world's second scientific revolution.

Modern science is now able to go well beyond looking at the atom as the basic building block of all things. Scientists have discovered that protons, neutrons, and electrons, which I had been taught were the smallest particles in the universe, are actually made up of even tinier sub-atomic particles— so small that they lose their identity as matter. Now, here comes the spooky part for me. Sub-atomic particles are not actually particles at all, at least not all the time. They are quanta of energy. It is not until they are observed by an outside entity, such as you or me, that they take form as matter. They exhibit all the qualities of wave energy until they are observed, at which point they become particles of matter.

Furthermore, mental activity, such as our thoughts, actually produces measurable energy, which affects the tiny subatomic particles that make up our universe. Consequently, we experience a world in which we, the observers, affect events that occur around us. In scientific terms, the observer has a measurable effect on an experiment, via a process of mental projection or, more accurately, through intention. In other words, our minds direct our ways of being in the world, of navigating our space, and of interacting with others, including animals.

Journalist Lynne McTaggart has researched and written two books on the quantum field and the power of intention. The first, *The Field, The Quest for the Secret Force of the Universe*, was later released as *The Field Updated*[x]. In this book, McTaggart identifies the many scientists who have worked diligently and meticulously to prove the existence of the quantum field and the manner in which a quanta of sub-atomic energy can be either a wave or a particle. In her second book, *The Intention Experiment*[xi], McTaggart documents the many exhaustive studies in which the intent of the observer affects the outcome of the experiment.

McTaggert's books gave me a clear, unshakable belief that there is a quantum energy field in which we are all connected. Within the field, our thoughts create measurable mental energy that then becomes part of the field. When this occurs, the mental or thought-energy can be instantaneously received by an observer at any distance from the originator. This energy can be picked up in a room in the same laboratory building or somewhere on the other side of the world. As such, thought energy in the quantum field can be used in communication, which means all sentient beings can connect with each other by this means — even one species to another.

At times, I still have trouble wrapping my brain around the concept. Then, I remember that had I lived six hundred years ago, I would have laughed at the idea of the earth being round and orbiting around the sun, or the idea that billions of stars and galaxies exist beyond our visual night sky. Had I lived two hundred years ago, the concept of flipping a switch on a wall and illuminating a room would have been pure black magic. Now, I perform that switch-flipping every day and think nothing of it. I may not know exactly how that happens or why it works, but I know that it does, in fact, work — every time. I can only speculate as to what new discoveries might be made in the future.

As I was first learning about animal communication, I was much more focused on how to do it rather than how it worked. I decided to, as the Nike commercial reads, "Just do it". However, this was going to necessitate a shift in how I was used to accomplishing difficult tasks.

As a naval aviator, I flew high-performance jets off aircraft carriers and in war zones. In my job as a commercial airline pilot, I thought nothing of flying a 747 from New York to Tokyo. One might say that engaging in such activities requires a healthy dose of self-confidence, i.e. ego. In fact, ego is a constructive and necessary component of accomplishing these tasks effectively. However, ego tends to speak a lot and is responsible for much of the continuous mental chatter that pervades our brains. Therefore, to dispense with that ego-based internal talk and simply listen to an animal, was, at least initially, a daunting process for me.

Then, when it was time to report back to the animal's person, my ego (in the form of self-consciousness and doubt) resurfaced. This was largely due to the discomfort of possibly being judged by people who may be skeptical about the validity of the communication. Disbelief is to be expected when people have not been exposed to the practice or borne witness to actual exchanges. Adding to my concern was the fact that I was new and unpracticed at the task. Even experienced animal communicators expect only an eighty to ninety percent accuracy rate so reporting to a doubter what that person's animal "said" filled me with a sense of unease. Quite frankly, I did not want to be mocked as a charlatan for doing something that I knew was real.

In the end, the animals won out. In our human-based world, animals have few rights and protections, and no voice. If those of us who are aware of their complex intellectual, emotional and psychological lives will not speak out for them, who will? With that in mind, I swallowed my ego (or at least suppressed it a little) and plunged ahead.

As with human exchange, there are various methods of speaking with animals, and I needed to develop a style that was comfortable for me. Some communicators visit the home or place where the animal lives. Others, such as my mentor Lisa Larson, communicate in real time, but not in the physical presence of the animal. This approach is analogous to simultaneous translation and occurs over the phone. In our sessions with Lisa, we are on the phone with her while she connects intuitively to the cats. We ask Lisa a question for the boys and she, in turn, asks them that question. She then relays their responses back to us. Still others, like Jeri Ryan, speak one on one with animals, and we are not part of the process. Jeri makes phone contact with us to find out what we would like to ask the boys. Then, off line, she subsequently speaks with each of them, and when that connection is complete, she calls back and tells us about the session. The last two methods do not require that the communicator be physically present with the animal. The communication can be done from the other side of town or the other side of the world. The zero-point energy field is unlimited and unrestricted by time or space.

Currently, I have adopted a method similar to Jeri Ryan's, which works very well for me. I ask the animal's guardian for a photo of the animal (which although not necessary assists me in focusing on the animal with whom I intend to connect), and a list of questions that they wish to ask. I meditate briefly, tune into the animal and make contact. After introducing myself to the animal and asking if I may talk with him/her, I ask a series of verification questions about things I don't know, but which can be readily confirmed by the animal's person. Examples might be "What is your favorite toy?" "What does your house look like?" "Where do you like to sleep?" and "Are there other animals living with you?". I will then proceed with the guardian's questions for the animal.

My first client was my daughter, Robin, who lives in Raleigh, North Carolina. Her beloved dog, Geo, was going to obedience school at the time. Robin wanted to know Geo's impressions and whether she enjoyed her training. Meditating on Geo, I tuned in and began asking the usual verification questions. In addition to asking what she thought of the training, I requested that she show me her instructor and the training facility. Robin had not told me anything about these topics, and I had not asked an animal to "show" me anything before, so this was new to me. However, I treated that request like the other questions and wrote down the first image that came to mind. I saw a tall woman with long blonde hair, and a brightly lit room with a white floor and fluorescent lighting. After recording my answers, I reported to Robin. "Wow!" Robin exclaimed. "That's exactly what the place looks like, and the trainer is a woman with long blonde hair!"

Evidently, Robin was impressed enough to tell her friend, Sharon, about the experience. Soon after, Sharon called upon me to speak with her cat Sweet Pea, who was not getting along with Buddy, one of her other cats. My communication with Sweet Pea made me realize just how much I still had to learn. Along with the typical verification questions, I asked Sweet Pea about her relationship with Buddy. She told me that he was very "bossy". In talking with Buddy, I learned that, according to him, he was in charge of the house, and whenever he told her to do something, Sweet Pea wouldn't listen. It turned out that Sweet Pea was new to the home, and there were issues as to who was in charge. Those issues eventually were resolved, but I had yet to re-learn another big lesson.

When I asked Sweet Pea what she enjoyed doing at home, she replied, "I like to sit on the chest and look out the window." To me, the word "chest" signifies the kind of travel chest seen in old-fashioned movies. These chests are only about two feet high, and therefore, a cat could not see out of a typical window when sitting on one. *She must mean a chest of drawers or a dresser,* I thought to myself. With doubts about my abilities teeming in my mind, I interpreted what Sweet Pea told me through my filters, and reported that she liked to sit on the dresser and look out the window.

Months later, when we visited Robin in Raleigh, we went to Sharon's home for the first time. There, in her dining room was a floor to ceiling window, looking out on her backyard. In front of the window was an old fashioned sea chest. Indeed, that was where Sweet Pea liked to spend her time, Sharon said. This case was similar to the boat communication, in that I had used my interpretation of the context of the conversation without simply relying on what the animal had to say. From then on, I tried very hard to take what I received from the animal, without interjecting my impressions or analysis. That was not an easy task since the animal's response comes into my awareness in the same "voice" as my own self-talk. That's when the art of interspecies communication comes into play, and I must distinguish between the animal's answer and my interpretation.

Another example of my learning process occurred during my communication with a horse named Cody. Cody had once lived in a corral with another horse. The two had become quite close, but the other horse had to be relocated. Cody's person wanted me to find out how he was faring. When I connected with Cody and asked him to "tell me about your buddy", he spoke to me about his best friend. He said that he talked to him, spent time with him and that they nuzzled each other. All references to his buddy were male. When I asked Cody to tell me his buddy's name, I received an indistinct answer, but it was a 'B' name (such as "Bill" or "Bob"). When I reported the conversation to Sherry, Cody's person, she told me that the other horse was a mare, named "Sylvia". *Wow!* I thought, *I was way off on that one.* Later in the conversation, Sherry told me about how her husband, Brian, had a very special relationship with Cody. He went to see Cody every day, nuzzled him, spoke with and spent time with him. It became very clear to me then that when I asked Cody about his "buddy", I was thinking of the other horse he used to live with. However, Cody was thinking of his current "buddy", the human, Brian (with the "B" name!).

My exchange with Cody was not unlike verbal communication between humans, in which two parties communicate but, at one point or another, are not on the same page. In that instance, one person intends to project a certain message that, for one reason or another, is interpreted by the listener to mean something else. Then, after a series of clarification questions, the listening party exclaims, "Oh, I thought you meant 'x', not 'y'!"

I also learned yet another important lesson about communication in general: to make sure the animal, the guardian, and I are all talking about the same thing at the same time. For instance, I once asked a cat named Charlie "What is your favorite food?" and received the answer, "I love chicken." When I reported that to the person, she replied, "Oh no, he only gets dry food." We eventually realized that dry food might be all he was getting to eat at that time, but he still loved the chicken best.

Another interesting aspect of intuitive communication occurred when I was asked to connect with the dog of a Hispanic woman. Rosa had been referred to me by a former client and wanted me to connect with her dog Pedro. Pedro had been living with Rosa's friend, but the friend had to move and could not take Pedro with her, so Pedro had just moved into Rosa's house. I was asked to talk with Pedro and let him know what was going on. Rosa told me their family spoke only Spanish in their home, as had been the case with her friend. It was the only human language Pedro had experienced. She wanted to know if Pedro could understand me, an English speaker, or if I would be able to understand him.

Communicating in the quantum field is not unlike having one of the universal translators worn by all of the characters in the science fiction series *Star Trek*. The spoken language does not matter as the communication is with thought energy. That energy is sent to the quantum field where it can be picked up by someone tuning into it, and that person or animal, in turn, puts that thought energy into a "language" they understand.

I had a nice conversation with Pedro and, while he was missing his former person and feeling sad about not being with her, he was able to understand the circumstances. I was able to convey to him that he was loved by her, and also loved by his new person Rosa and that he would be safe and cared for in his new home.

Sometimes communications can be humorous, if a little embarrassing for the guardian. I was asked to connect with Gracie, a beautiful German Shepard and in the course of the conversation, asked her what she like to eat. "Oh, I like the dry crunchy food, and sometimes I get wet food, but I like 'people food' the best," Gracie told me. The wife seemed surprised and said, "I don't know why she says 'people food' because she never gets any of that." It was the husband who shyly confessed that frequently he feeds Gracie "people food", even though he knows he's not supposed to.

With virtually every one of my clients, an "a-ha!" moment occurs – a point of acknowledgment that animal communication is, in fact, real. For example, one of my referrals requested that I speak with Bellina, her female cat. One of the verification questions I posed was, "What is your favorite toy?" "I love to play with the red dot," Bellina replied. When I relayed this answer, I could hear an intake of breath (the classic "a-ha!" moment) and my client exclaimed, "Yes, yes! We play with the laser pointer every evening!"

The emotional impact and surprise at an accurate reading is always rewarding. I am still quite amazed and delighted at the joy I sense on the part of humans when they realize their animal friend is actually communicating with them through my connection with them in the quantum field.

CHAPTER 13

VOICES OF COMPASSION
AND REASON

Animals not only hear us, speak to us, and communicate their feelings, they also care deeply and worry about their humans. They pick up on our feelings and states of mind, and they can be profoundly influenced by what is going on in our lives. The following stories illustrate the interconnectedness of animal and human lives.

Once, when I was part of a tour group traveling in Peru, one of my traveling companions (whom I will call "Brenda") sat next to me at lunch, looking very forlorn. I had not known Brenda prior to this tour and only established a casual acquaintanceship with her as the tour progressed. When I asked her what was wrong, Brenda told me that she and her husband had decided to euthanize one of their four cats. The cat, named Sable, had been acquired when she was a kitten and had lived with them for eight years. Apparently, Sable had a problem with aggression toward the other cats in the household, to such a degree that the situation had become unmanageable. Brenda was visibly upset. She had spoken with her husband back in Wisconsin, and they had decided he would take Sable to the vet to be euthanized while Brenda was still on the tour. In that way, Brenda would not have to be part of the actual process. I tried to calm her down by saying that putting Sable down was not the only solution. After a long conversation, I persuaded Brenda to allow me to speak with Sable. Initially, there was a bit of eye-rolling involved on Brenda's part, but I also sensed that there was a glimmer of hope.

The first step was for Brenda to call her husband in Wisconsin, and tell him not to go through with their plans for Sable. I asked Brenda to send me a photo of the cat, so as to make the initial connection. About two days after the trip ended, I received a picture of the sweet soul with whom I would connect.

Once I made contact with Sable, I asked my confirmations questions first. Then, I asked what was going on in the house amongst the cats, referencing her aggressive behavior. Sable replied, "That's a cat thing. It is not your problem." I then let her know that if the aggression continued, and there wasn't any peace in the house, there would be consequences, one of which was that she would not be able to live there anymore (of course, I didn't tell her the true nature of Brenda's plans). "Brenda needs to have a calm, loving household," I explained gently. "The home should be pleasant, safe, and happy for everyone. The fighting must stop. If not, you will have to leave."

The latter statement caught Sable's attention. Suddenly, she realized that there was a very troublesome issue going on, and she would have to change her ways or lose her home and her people. She told me how much she loved Brenda and was deeply distressed that she might have to leave. After some more conversation, she decided she would work to change things. Our conversations continued every three to four months over the next year, during which time there were alternate periods of progress and regression. Whenever Sable acted aggressively, Brenda would become upset again and call me in a state of anxiety. In those stressful times, I explained that heightened tensions on Brenda's part were counterproductive, and that she (Brenda) had to calm her own energy, interact rationally and peacefully with her cats, and separate them when the aggression occurred.

To my delight, Brenda sent me a photo this past summer, depicting all four of her cats, eating peacefully and calmly, side by side at their food bowls. It was so gratifying for me actually to see the positive results of intuitive communication with Sable and to know that together we had, in some measure, facilitated the prevailing peace in Brenda's home.

An illustration of explicitly expressed animal devotion was the case of Abby, a beautiful Labrador, and her person, Rick. Abby was old and ill, and Rick was not sure whether it was time for her to pass away. He wanted to get Abby's thoughts on the subject, and contacted me to connect with her. After posing the usual straightforward, verifiable questions, I asked Abby how she felt.

"Not well," she answered.

"What's wrong?" I inquired.

"My back," she responded.

"If your back were fixed, would you be OK?" I pressed further.

"No, other parts hurt," she informed me.

"Do you want to pass?" I asked.

"Rick would be sad," Abby said soulfully.

"When it is time for you to leave your body, do you want help from the vet? Should Rick ask the vet to help you when it's time?" I questioned, with tears welling in my eyes.

"Yes, but I'm not ready," Abby said. "I'm so concerned that Rick will be sad."

"How will you let Rick know when it's time?" My words came slowly, as I swallowed hard.

"When I don't want to go on my walk. When I no longer respond when Rick wants to take me on walks, that will be the sign" Abby told me.

"Is there anything else that you want Rick to know?" I asked.

"I just don't want Rick to be sad. I want him to remember the happy times, how much fun we had, and what a great life we had together. I love the sound of his laughter," Abby concluded.

About five months later, I got a call from Rick. For the first time ever, Abby had refused to go for a walk. Rick recognized the signal and knew that it was, definitely, time. Abby transitioned, and although Rick's heart was heavy, he knew that Abby had a say in the matter and was very grateful that he did not have to agonize over the decision. He also expressed deep gratitude that they had been able to have those last five months together.

For my part, I was somewhat surprised at the very deep emotion I felt when connecting with Abby. Several of the books I have read about animal communication have stressed that a feeling of deep emotion is an unmistakable sign that the communicator is in direct contact with the animal. It was a sure indication to me I was operating from my "heart" and not in my "head". Abby's thoughts about Rick were being sent to me and translated in my brain into human language. In the same way, her emotions about Rick were also being transmitted to me, and the love and devotion she had for "her person" reached deep into my soul and moved me to tears. To this day, this case still stirs profound feelings in me, as I continue to encounter the love and empathy that animals can have for their human friends.

A similar scenario occurred with a dog named Levi and his people, Barry and Rhonda. On a night when Levi seemed to be very close to death, Barry called and asked me to connect with him. Levi was ill and knew that it was time for him to transition, but realizing how bereaved Barry and Rhonda would be upon his passing, he wanted to stay an extra day or two. Levi stayed for another day, then gave Barry a pre-arranged sign, and was helped out of his pain-wracked body. When Levi had left his body and was in spirit, Barry called and asked me to contact Levi "on the other side".

All life exists as a quanta of energy in the vast quantum field — the basis of our universe. Physical life as we know it may end, but the energy of each being is indestructible. At the zero-point energy of the quantum field, all energy forms can continue to connect, and it is in this realm that I communicated with Levi, as I have with other animals, before and since. Barry wanted to inquire about his transition and whether he had a good experience and was happy. Levi confirmed that, indeed, he was content. When I asked Levi if he continued to visit his people, and if Barry and Rhonda could feel his presence around the house, he emphatically replied, "Yes!" He said he was around them all the time. Barry confirmed this, saying that he and Rhonda felt Levi around them many times and sensed that they could share their love and affection with each other across the divide of physical existence.

Another illustration of the interplay of emotions between animals and their people came to light for me when Margaret called to ask for my help with her cat, Lucy. Lucy had been excessively over-grooming and removing her fur down to the skin. Margaret wondered what the source of this neurotic behavior could be. Was it physical, dietary, an allergic reaction, or something else? Deeply concerned, she called me to connect with Lucy and find out what was causing this behavior. My first response was to tell Margaret to take Lucy to a vet and find out if there was a physical cause for the over grooming. At Lucy's vet visit, all of those factors were ruled out. According to the vet, Lucy had a "psychological problem".

Margaret again asked for my intervention, and I gladly spoke with Lucy. After some initial introductions and talk, I said:

"Lucy, it looks like you are licking away a lot of your fur."

"Yeah, some of it." She replied.

"I think it's lots of it." I said.

"Yeah, maybe."

"I want you to have a full, healthy coat of fur. That means only licking to clean yourself." I told her.

"Sometimes I'm just bored. Sometimes I'm nervous." She replied.

"Do you know what makes you nervous?" I asked.

"I don't know. Margaret gets nervous and that makes me nervous. I think I upset her. I make her angry and make things bad for her. I don't think she likes me."

I assured Lucy that Margaret loved her very much and wanted her to be healthy and happy. As I reported this conversation to Margaret, I learned that she had come upon some tough times. She was very stressed, embroiled in complex personal and work relationships, and was experiencing serious self-esteem issues. As a result, she took her frustrations out on Lucy, alternately shouting at her, even when Lucy engaged in normal cat behavior, or completely ignoring her. Consequently, Lucy was absorbing much of Margaret's distress, which manifested itself in the cat's abnormal behavior.

Upon hearing Lucy's frustrations, Margaret had an "a-ha!" moment and began to realize how her emotional state affected that of her companion. No longer did she view Lucy as simply a blob of fur, whom she could dominate and on whom she could take out her frustrations. Rather, Margret saw her as an intelligent, complex, emotionally and psychologically sentient being, whose life was inextricably entwined with her own.

Over the next few years, after several connections with Lucy and a lot of self-reflection on Margaret's part, things gradually changed. By no means was there an instantaneous "healing", but rather a long slow progression. Margaret realized that she had to take ownership of her difficulties, and diffuse the negative energy in her life. She needed help, and once she found her center, she was able to mend her relationship with Lucy and live in mutual peace, joy, and fulfillment. Lucy had served as Margaret's teacher and helped her to find solace and equilibrium in her world.

Our animal companions provide us with unique ways of giving and receiving love. As I have learned in my experience, the voices of love and compassion come in all sizes, shapes, forms, colors, and stripes. We just have to open our minds and hearts to feel the vibrations of Divine Love reverberating within all of us.

CHAPTER 14

THE CAT WHISPERER

When dealing with people who seek my intervention as an animal communicator (particularly when communicating with cats), I'm often asked the interesting question, "Are you a cat whisperer?" In truth, I don't have a firm answer. Because I have communicated with animals of all kinds, including (but not limited to) cats, dogs, horses, tigers, elephants, zonkeys (crosses between zebras and donkeys), camels, snakes, birds, fish, insects, and a squirrel, I am not a "whisperer" of any specific species of animal. However, because I live with cats and have studied them extensively, I can make suggestions about how to accommodate and harmonize feline and human interaction. In that sense, therefore, I guess I can say that I'm a "cat whisperer" of sorts.

The word "whisperer" entered pop culture with the release of the 1998 film, *The Horse Whisperer*, starring Robert Redford. The movie was based on Nicholas Evans' novel of the same name. In Evans' story the whisperer was a composite of three actual men, the most prominent of whom was Buck

Brannaman. The book deals with a horse named "Pilgrim" who was in a very severe accident and subsequently begins to act aggressively toward humans. Pilgrim faces possible euthanasia, until a trainer, Tom Booker (played by Redford), enters his life. The "horse whisperer" becomes in tune with Pilgrim's feelings and fears, and over time, re-establishes the trust between the horse and humans. It is important to note that Booker connects at Pilgrim's level of understanding and willingness to continue the relationship, not at the human level of expectation. After the film's release, the term "whisperer" entered our vernacular, signifying "anyone with a strong affinity for a particular animal or species".

Later, the television show *The Dog Whisperer* starring Cesar Millan aired on the National Geographic channel. On the show, Cesar would go to the home of a person with a "problem dog" (that is, the dog would engage in excessive barking, aggression, destructive chewing, etc.) and observe the interaction between the dog and its guardian. Through his method of understanding the dog's instinctive needs, he could determine why the dog was acting as it was and make corrections to the behavior. He would then enlighten the human guardians as to why the dog acted in a particular manner. He also made it clear the dog was in some way reflecting the person's emotional state, and tell the human how he/she had to change to alter the dog's behavior. Cesar became noted for saying that he "rehabilitated dogs and trained people". The series ended in 2012 but currently, as of this writing, a new show with a similar format, *Cesar 911*, airs on the National Geographic Wild channel

In his first book, *Cesar's Way*[xii], Cesar tells of his birth and upbringing in rural Mexico, and how he was always around and interacting with dogs. He entered the U.S. illegally (he has since earned his citizenship) and was only able to obtain employment as a dog groomer. His ability to connect with dogs quickly gained attention, and he began working with "problem dogs" to cure behavioral issues. He discovered that the vast majority of problems were caused by dog owners who had very little understanding of dogs, their instincts, and how they interact with the world around them.

Another program on the Animal Planet channel addresses feline-human interaction: *My Cat From Hell*, starring Jackson Galaxy. The show offers a format akin to *The Dog Whisperer*. In each show, Jackson goes to the homes of people with a "problem cat". He observes the people, the cat, the environment and their interaction and suggests ways in which to make the household more harmonious.

In his book, *Cat Daddy*[xiii], Jackson writes about his former job at the Humane Society of Boulder, Colorado where one of his tasks was to euthanize stray cats. The process tore him apart emotionally, and he decided to dedicate his life to healing human/feline conflicts. Jackson does not use the term "whisperer" but refers to himself as a "cat behaviorist".

Both of these programs point out that all too often, people want their animals to adapt to human conceptions of how the animal should behave. This approach is not beneficial to either the animal or the human guardian. Cats cannot behave like dogs and dogs cannot behave like cats, and neither can act as humans. Instead, humans should be able to recognize their animals' instinctive species-based needs and accommodate them.

An example of an instinctive behavior is a cats' search for the litter box and the burying of their waste, without being taught. Their predecessors in the Sahara desert of Northern Africa (where the species may have originated) lived in sandy soil. As small animals, who were both predator and prey (i.e., they were the hunters and the hunted), burying their waste became a survival behavior, so as not to be detected by their predators through their scent trails. Such behavior was passed down through the generations of wild or feral cats until it became instinctive. As cats became domesticated, the instinct was passed on to house cats like Oscar, who has meticulously buried his waste from the beginning of his time with us, without any training whatsoever.

Cats also have a penchant for patrolling their territory, checking out every spot to ascertain whether changes have occurred. Any alteration in their territory can indicate the presence of a possible predator in the area. If something or someone new enters their environs, they approach the foreign object or perceived invader very cautiously, sniffing for potential dangers. When I was child, such displays of caution would label one a "'fraidy cat". For many cats, past and present, this behavior is a matter of life or death, ingrained in cats' basic make-up.

According to the Merriam-Webster dictionary, instinct or innate behavior is defined as "A natural or inherent aptitude, impulse, or capacity. A largely inheritable and unalterable tendency of an organism to make a complex and specific response to environmental stimuli without involving reason."

The above-referenced definition indicates instinct is not learned behavior, but rather, inherent in the underlying physiological make-up of the organism. Much of cats' behavior is evolutionary, and not a product of chance. For instance, when faced with danger, a cat will arch its back, puff out its fur, turn sideways to the source of danger, and hiss. In so doing, the cat looks larger and much more menacing. Therefore, the assertive cat has a better chance of survival (and thus, passing on its genes) than a docile cat, who may shrink down and try to look small. So, throughout history, cats who adopted this assertive behavior survived more frequently and procreated. In turn, their offspring learned the behavior, which continued to be passed down to successive generations. Eventually, the behavior became instinctive.

Interestingly, in the human realm, we tend to believe that we can override instinctive behaviors; that we can reason, analyze, and learn certain modes of behavior that cancel out some of our fundamental instincts. Despite this belief, we still maintain these behaviors and feelings. One of the most common is called the "flight or fight syndrome". When faced with potential danger, we almost always react with one or the other of these actions. Even if we override the instinct and do nothing, the physiological response remains and the body manufactures stress homones.

There is much debate about how a learned behavior becomes an instinct. The famous psychiatrist Carl Jung (1875–1961) believed all beings had a collective unconscious which was shared among beings of the same species and was populated by instincts and archetypes. Other famous philosophers from Aristotle to Descartes have argued about what instincts are and where they come from.

As I have continued to learn about the quantum field and the basic ideas of the second scientific revolution, I have to wonder if it is this connection to the quantum field that provides life forms with what we call "instinct". I have come to believe that the quantum field is that vast source of Divine Intelligence infused in all beings and encompassing absolutely everything. After all bees build hives, birds build nests and spiders build webs, all done without benefit of instruction or observation. Where do the instincts to do these things come from?

Perhaps, to survive in the world, all beings tap into that part of the quantum energy field where the intelligence source provides them with guidance as to what to do and how to act — behaviors specific to their species. For humans, we sometimes call this following our "gut" feelings. We might say we have an instinctive "feel" for how we should handle new situations. The most striking example of this type of feeling for me is the emotional thunderbolt which struck me and indicated that Oscar was to stay with us!

So, what is the distinction between animal communication and animal-whispering, and how do the two impact the relationships between animals and humans? I have observed that, in the case of whisperers and behaviorists, no conscious attempt is made to establish two-way communications with the animal. They base their work on their understanding of specific species' needs, propensities, and tendencies. In so doing, they can usually resolve behavioral issues effectively. They do not ask or seek input from the individual animal. Another considerable distinction is that a behaviorist usually works with only one species, whereas a communicator works with all sentient beings.

A behaviorist may look for the reasons why a particular behavior occurs, and then attempt to change the conditions that cause the behavior. As a communicator, I tend to focus more on what the animal is thinking or feeling about a situation and try to view events from that animal's perspective. I always remember the early conversation Jeri Ryan had with Oliver when Oliver pooped outside the litter box. She started by saying "Oliver, we have a problem. Can you help us? Someone is pooping outside the litter box. Could it be you?" She did not accuse him of anything, or ask why, she asked for his help. Next, after Oliver had said it was he, she said, "There must be a reason. Can you tell me what it is?" It was not until after Oliver had explained his reasoning that she impressed on him that pooping outside the box was extremely upsetting to us.

I rarely ask an animal "why" it does something. Frequently, as with humans, an animal may not know why it behaves in a particular manner. Rather, I inquire about the behavior itself or a given pattern of conduct. The intention of communication is to understand the animal's point of view and to be an advocate for them, rather than induce a behavior change (although the change may, in fact, come about). This assessment does not, in any way, suggest that one mode of engagement is more effective or valuable than the other. In my opinion, they are different, although co-related.

The importance of allowing our four-legged (or winged or finned) family members to simply *be*, without having to conform to our human conceptions of how they should act in order to accommodate our lifestyles, cannot be overemphasized. This does not mean our animals should be completely free to "do their thing", whatever it may be. Just as humans must adjust their lives to live with animals, animals must sometimes adjust to live with their people.

Indeed, dogs and cats alike can be taught to respond to commands so as to accommodate our sharing of living space. These kinds of behaviors are vital in promoting the animal's well-being, as well as providing structure in their human guardians' environment. An example of this in our house is that cats are not allowed on the dining room table or the kitchen counter. Their paws track through the cat litter, and while the enzymes in their bodies may guard them from ill effects of any residue they may pick up there, our human enzymes do not offer us the same protection. So the few times they have attempted to explore these regions, we tell them "paws on the floor", and if necessary, physically move them off the surface.

Sometimes, however, humans cross way over the line when dictating the course of animal lives. The practice of declawing cats (which is, in reality, toe amputation) is a cruel and inhumane form of altering a cat's physical state. Unlike a human finger nail, a cat's claws are connected to their muscles and tendons, up through the legs and shoulders. This is what enables the cat to extend and retract its claws. In order to remove the claw, the toe must be amputated at the first joint. After the painful process of amputation the cat must adapt to the change in its musculoskeletal framework. It must learn to run and walk on its paw pads instead of on its toes, as it normally does. This changes and affects the cat's entire balance and cripples it for life. It will also be unable to stretch properly and may have trouble using the litter box (the sandy clay-based soil used in many brands of litter feels painful on the nubs of the cat's toes when it digs). Additionally, the cat will lose its ability to climb. Further, there is psychological damage that occurs, in that the cat loses its primary form of defense.

Many veterinarians don't reveal the devastating effects of toe amputation, since the people who want the procedure are usually so insistent, that if their vet doesn't comply, they will seek another doctor. Sadly, in an attempt to preserve their furniture and prevent scratches, many people opt for toe amputation, without realizing that they are permanently maiming their cat.

There are other ways in which to accomplish the objective of keeping the household furniture intact, without resorting to such a devastating procedure. Scratching posts, for example, help a cat to get rid of residue on its claws while serving as an excellent place to reach up and stretch. Cats can be trained to use their scratching posts through intuitive communication and outright praise when the cat adheres to a given request. "Use your scratching post, Oscar!" I remind my buddy when he begins to glance at the chair or sofa as a scratching device. Of course, every time we see him or his brothers using a post or scratching pad, we make sure that we praise them. Even Obe Juan, as he aged, would make a point to use the scratching posts, and then look to us for acknowledgment of his good behavior.

Whisperers and communicators both work toward the same goal: to make the human- animal interface a smooth and harmonious experience for both species. This is, in fact, what it means to be a communicator and a whisperer - know the animal, understand the kind of positive reinforcement to which it will respond, and make the effort to learn about the species. Anyone can do it. All it takes is compassion, willingness, and an open mind.

CHAPTER 15

COMMUNICATING
WITH YOUR ANIMAL

There is a distinction between communicating *with* and talking *to* your animal. While one is usually considered to be a two way process, the other is generally thought to be a one way sending out of information. Two way communication may be ideal, but just the realization that an animal is an intelligent being with a capacity to understand us can enrich and strengthen our bonds with our animal families.

Earlier in the book I wrote about my education in learning about stilling my mind with meditation, visualizing energy flow, then asking questions and writing down answers. It took the reading of many books, some training seminars, and lots and lots of practice for me to learn to communicate effectively with animals. Not everyone has the time or inclination to do all of that, but each one of us can go a long way toward establishing closer bonds with our animals by learning a few of the basics.

According to Merriam-Webster, the word "communicate" comes from the Latin word *communicatus* meaning "to impart, participate". The term is defined as "the act or process of using words, sounds, signs or behaviors to express or exchange information or to express your ideas, thoughts, feelings, etc. to someone else."

In layman's terms, there are three steps to communication.

(1) Thought: First, information exists in the mind of the sender. This can be a concept, idea, information or feeling.

(2) Sending: Next, a message is sent to a receiver via words or other symbols.

(3) Decoding: Lastly, the receiver translates the words or symbols into a concept or information that a person can understand.

In graduate school I learned the concept of Neural Linguistic Programing (NLP), which posits that communication is further affected by each individual's inborn, preferred method of processing information. These methods are based on our five physical senses, so while I may process information primarily in visual terms, someone else might process information aurally or tactilely.

While these are useful "book" definitions and concepts, they deal only with exchanges between humans. The definitions offered do not refer to telepathy or intuitive thought, and certainly not to energy exchange in the quantum field. I believe we should include the idea that communication involves the transmission of ideas from the consciousness of one sentient being to that of another sentient being. Ideally, this type of communication should be mutual, with each party sending and receiving.

However, many people are still unaware that animals are sentient, intelligent beings, and they have no clue that the animals are sending thoughts out to them. If people do understand this, they sometimes don't believe that they can receive and comprehend what their animal is telling them. This is understandable because as mentioned before, the animal's transmissions usually come to us "sounding" like our inner voice. The overwhelming temptation is just to assume that we are making stuff up, and that transmissions from our animals are more wishful thinking on our part than actual intelligent communication.

I experienced a stunning example of how strongly an animal can communicate with his person when he needs to. A few years ago Catherine and I were spending a weekend get-away with our good friends Barry and Rhonda in a house on an inlet in Northern California. They had brought their dog Levi (who you met in a previous chapter) with them. The four of us humans were gathered in the kitchen while Levi was running loose, playing in the back yard. As we were chatting about something, Rhonda stopped in mid-sentence, looked at us all in shock and asked urgently, "Where's Levi?". None of us had heard a noise or had any indication that something was wrong, but Rhonda was getting a clear, strong feeling that she needed to find Levi. We all rushed out to the back yard to discover Levi had fallen into the water in an area where there was a sea wall and he could not get out. He was swimming to stay afloat, but tiring quickly and could not touch bottom. Barry was able to jump in and save him, but without Levi's intuitive call for help, and Rhonda's reception of that call, it could have been a disaster. At that time, Rhonda knew very little about animal communication, but her connection to Levi and that strong message he was sending her was enough to allow her to "hear" his call for help.

In my experience, most pet guardians are aware that their animals do, in fact, possess intelligence — or at least a degree of intelligence that could result in meaningful communication. People often tell me, "I speak to my animals all the time, and I know that they hear and understand me." The fact that animals hear what their people tell them is certainly accurate, but understanding what their people mean depends not on the words coming from our mouths, but on the thoughts in our minds. Therefore, if we are saying one thing but thinking or feeling something else, we are, at best, sending a mixed message and, at worst, making our animal neurotic. Since our human method of communication with each other is verbal, we almost always accompany our thoughts to our animals with spoken words. This becomes tricky, at times, because that which we transmit to our animals mentally is sometimes not exactly what we want to convey.

A classic example is the use of negative terms. Let's say your cat scratches the furniture. As I noted before, scratching is an innate behavior, necessary for stretching muscles and the shedding of the claw-sheath from cats' claws. If we don't provide a place for cats to accomplish this necessary task (e.g., scratching posts), they will use anything else at their disposal: the sofa, chairs, the carpet, etc.

So, let's suppose that you don't have a scratching post. When your cat approaches the sofa, you call out "Don't scratch the sofa!" As you utter these words, squirt water or yell "No!", you have an image in your mind of the cat scratching the sofa. The cat, in turn, doesn't hear "don't" or "no". Rather, it picks up on your visual imaging and sees itself scratching the sofa

— engaging in the very behavior that you wish to modify. The mixed message is extremely confusing to the cat, which sees an image of him/herself in your mind, scratching the sofa, while you are shouting "No!" and forbidding the very activity that is being pictured in your brain. Therefore, it is much more useful to send the cat a picture of the behavior that we want.

First, make sure there are many "approved" scratching surfaces available (such as scratching posts or pads, which are readily available in all pet stores), placed where the cat is likely to scratch. Then, form an image in your mind of the cat using one of these surfaces, and say to the cat, "Use your scratching post." Instead of using negative terms (which rarely have the desired effect), state your desired behavior (i.e., that which you want to occur).

It is also interesting to note our human sub-conscious mind does not process negative statements very well. Telling ourselves "don't smoke" or "don't eat that second piece of chocolate cake" has much less effect than re-enforcing the positive ideas we do want: "I have clean, clear lungs", or "I choose to eat healthy food." The animal's brain does not process negatives either, and the visual picture in our brains of behaviors that we do not want the animal to engage in actually promotes that very behavior.

An example of canine behavioral modification is the "two-bark rule". Dogs are pack animals, and bark to alert others of impending dangers, intruders, or potential changes in the environment. People often request that I attempt to modify excessive barking tendencies in dogs. Telling a dog "Don't bark" will have little effect because to say these words, we have to formulate a mental picture of the dog barking. Again, the rule is to send a picture of the behavior that we *do* want, not the opposite. Therefore, we can say "Be silent" or, since the dog usually has to bark to warn the pack (i.e., us), we can say, "Two barks, and then you must be quiet." Sending the telepathic message that the dog should bark only twice will enable the animal carry out its instinctive need, while modifying the undesirable behavior. We can do this with virtually any behavior we want to modify. Instead of using the command "Don't jump on people", we can say "All paws on the floor". Instead of saying "Don't chew on my slippers", we can say "Chew only on your chew toys".

It is important to mention that if our animals do not adhere to our request, that doesn't mean that they don't understand or aren't listening. The animal may have an ingrained habit that will take time to modify. Additionally, the animal may have reasons for engaging in a particular behavior that, to him/her, makes perfect sense, but is not immediately comprehensible to us. If that is the case, the human must investigate and understand the cause of the animal's behavior.

Some behaviors, however, are non-negotiable. Our cats, for example, are indoors only and not allowed outside. It is simply too dangerous for them. So, when we approach the door to leave, instead of saying "Don't go out", we say, "Stay back". When we return and find them waiting a couple of feet from the door, we make sure that we praise their "beautiful waiting", and send out feelings of pleasure in response to their behavior.

Another non-negotiable behavior is a cat's use of the litter box at all times. A cat's failure to do so indicates that something is going on which is causing a deviation from an instinctive behavior. When a cat does not use the litter box, some humans may be tempted to label the cat "bad", but a deviation from instinctive behavior has much deeper roots than the superficial labels of either "good" or "bad". The root cause could be a medical issue with the cat or an environmental issue (a poorly placed litter box or litter which is not good for the cat, due to odor or feel). Perhaps a strange outdoor cat is triggering territorial instincts. Saying "bad cat" or inflicting punishment by squirting the cat with water or swatting with a newspaper will only cause confusion and trauma. Some people might still believe the old wives tale that rubbing the animal's nose in excrement will cure the problem. This is a horrible thing to do to any creature. Animals have no concept of punishment. They cannot relate our use of punitive measures to the behavior that we wish to modify. Therefore, the result of punishment signifies — from animals' perspectives — the loss of trust and love.

To return to the either-or notions of "good" and "bad". These terms, I have come to believe, have no validity whatsoever, not just in animal behavioral issues but in life, in general. Events are simply occurrences and our perceptions of them give rise to our usage of the terms "good" and "bad". One of my favorite writings is from the Rumi (1207-1273) the Sufi mystic and poet who wrote "Beyond our ideas of right-doing and wrong-doing, there is a field. I'll meet you there."

This brings me to a story that I first heard in church long ago. The tale involves a peasant farmer who was considered very well-off because he owned a horse. One day, the horse got out and ran off. Many of his neighbors came by to commiserate with him and comment on such a terrible situation.

"What bad luck!" they said.

"Perhaps," the farmer replied.

A week later, the horse returned, leading two other horses with him. So now the farmer owned three horses. The neighbors came by and exclaimed "How lucky you are! What good fortune!"

"Perhaps," the farmer responded.

A week later, the farmer's son was training one of the new horses, when he was thrown off and broke his leg.

"What bad luck!" the neighbors cried.

"Perhaps," the farmer answered.

Another week passed. The Army came through the village and drafted all the young men to go away and fight, but because the farmer's son had a broken leg, he could not go.

"What good luck!" said the neighbors.

The story can continue ad infinitum but, of course, the point is that none of the events were either "good" or "bad". They were, simply, a natural consequence of living. Humans tend to assign labels to events and judge them as being either one of two extremes — "good" or "bad". Animals, in contrast, don't have labels (i.e., concepts of "good" or "bad"), and they don't place judgments on anything. They just do what they must at any given time.

Habitual practices are often difficult to change — for animals, as well as for humans. For humans, smoking or over-eating are habitual practices that many people must work very hard to overcome. Getting a young child to put dirty clothes in the hamper instead of on the floor drives many parents to distraction. Likewise, persuading a cat to change to a new cat food or a dog to not chew the newspaper can be a challenge.

I don't know if I have ever had an animal actually lie to me about anything, but I remember working with a cat named Sophie, who was known to stretch the truth about her habitual behavior of chewing. She would chew and swallow fabrics and then have to be taken to the vet to clean out her system. I talked to her and she assured me she would not do that any longer. Except she did. So I talked to her again.

"You chewed on a lot of things Sophie," I said.

"Yes, I like to chew on things," she answered

"Do you still chew on things?"

"Well," she said, "not really."

"I don't understand," I persisted, "what do you mean?"

"Well, I nibble. But, I don't chew things up," she told me.

Her distinction between chewing and nibbling is a very fine line I'm not sure I concur with. In Sophie's mind however, there is a distinction.

I cannot over-emphasize my belief that the best and most efficient way to change behavior is with positive re-enforcement. Giving praise or rewards for behaviors we wish to instill in our animals is a win-win situation. One of the best ways animal communicators and trainers have found to do this is with "clicker training", a method developed by Karen Pryor and explained in her book *Reaching the Animal Mind*[xiv]. When a positive behavior takes place, it is rewarded with a "click" and a treat of food. The click can be either from a small handheld clicker, or even just a clicking noise in the mouth. Eventually, the human can do away with the treat and just use a click to reward their animal friend. This method can also be used to teach tricks to the animal. Our boys have learned to sit, shake hands (paws), lie down and sit up, all by using clicker training.

Learning to communicate with our animals is also an essential element of maintaining their mental wellbeing. Sometimes we need to talk to our companions to let them know about events that will affect them. My daughter Robin and her husband Bryan adopted a parrot, Bailey, shortly after they married. Seven years later, circumstances had changed and for Bailey's sake, they decided to find him a different home. Thirteen years later Bailey's new people were in a situation where Bailey was alone in his cage most of the time, so since Robin's life style had changed and they were much better equipped to give Bailey a good home, it was decided he would be returned to Robin and Bryan, who now also had three kids and a dog. I was asked to talk with Bailey about the upcoming changes in his life. After the initial introduction and pleasantries, I said:

"Bailey, do you remember Robin and Bryan?'

"Of course, my people," he replied.

"Well, Bailey, you're going to go back and live with them again," I informed him.

"Wow! Really? I like them. But what about my people here?" he asked.

I was struck with his concern for his current family and informed him that they were sad at giving him up, but felt bad that he was now having to spend almost all of his time alone in his cage.

"Yes, I really am lonely sometimes. It will be really nice to be around people. I like being around people," he told me.

"There are others living with them now. Three children and dog," I said.

"Children? I don't know about this. Kids always poke fingers at me. Lots of humans do, but kids are the worst. I don't like that." He explained.

I explained to him the children were mature and had great respect for animals and were really looking forward to giving him a great home. I went on to tell him when and how the transfer would take place and that he would go on a trip in his cage in a truck, which would probably be bumpy and loud, but that he would then arrive at his new home and be loved and cared for for the rest of his life.

The transfer took place and Bailey is now back with Robin, Bryan, and his new family members. He enjoys taking turns sitting on the shoulders of each of the family. He also likes and gets along with Geo, his new dog friend.

This is a rather dramatic change in life events, but the same concept applies to our animals for just about anything that affects them. If someone is coming to be a house guest, or the animal is going to go to a kennel while we travel, these are things which we should communicate to our animals. It is the same thing we would do for our human family members: to let them know of events that are going to affect their lives.

No discussion about communicating with your animal would be complete without mentioning concepts of time. People often ask me if animals can tell time. The answer is yes, although not in the same way humans do. Animals cannot count five days or ten hours, but they do have a sense of time's passage, especially when humans communicate it to them. When leaving an animal alone while you go somewhere, it is always a good idea to let the animal know you are leaving, you are coming home in a certain amount of time, and then sending a thought of how happy you will be when you return and greet your animal. Most people when leaving home for a while would tell the people they live with they are going. It seems fair to show our animals the same courtesy.

When we leave home, Catherine and I say to our cats "We'll be back in a few hours. Be good, take care of the house and each other. See you later. Thank you." While our boys do not necessarily pick up on how long we will be away, they sense our brains' thought processes, know that we are going out and will return. When we go away on long trips, we take photographs of them with us and send thought waves of love every day that we are absent from home. We also give them a countdown of how long until our return (e.g., "We will be home with you in five more days."). Of course, our cats are not necessarily going to count to five, but we transmit a concept of that amount of time in our brains, which they can sense.

It is worth mentioning that frequently, when we want more accurate two-way communication about important situations, Catherine and I will ask other communicators to talk with our boys. We know them so well and have a sense of how they might respond or what we would like the response to be, plus their answers to our questions always come to us sounding like our own self-talk. It can be hard to determine what their voice and thought is, and what we may be projecting as their thoughts. Most communicators we know will ask another professional to speak with their animals about important issues for the same reason. Introducing a third party into the process gives us much more accuracy and objectivity.

When we put thought-energy out into the quantum field, animals grasp our mental images both while sleeping and awake. Thus, it doesn't matter if they are napping when we communicate our messages and intentions. At the most fundamental level of the zero-point energy of the quantum field they are always listening and aware.

Communicating with your animal does not even have to be for a specific purpose. Sometimes just sharing time and space together and sharing feelings of companionship is all that is wanted. I have also been surprised at how many animals have told me they would like their people to sing to them because they just like the sound of their voice. Many animals tell me how they love the sound of their person's laughter.

It is exciting to realize that all of us can communicate with animals via mental images and telepathic messages. If words also accompany our thoughts, that is fine; but it is important to remember animals process mental pictures, not verbal language. Therefore, we must make sure that we develop the correct mental image of the thought we want to send them – something affirmative, rather than negative. Our task is to be sure that we send the actual message that we want them to "hear".

CHAPTER 16

OSCAR, THE WONDER CAT

There is no doubt that Oscar was the *CAT*alyst for my understanding of the inherent cognitive, emotional and psychological intelligence of animals. In fact, his presence in my life has given me renewed perspective on virtually everything. The universe is an amazing place, teeming with life forms, each with a unique and extraordinary intelligence of their own. Often, however, we humans believe that we have dominion over the earth — that, somehow, we are "superior" to all other beings with whom we share our planet. That was what I was taught. However, as my understanding of the quantum field has grown, I now believe that this notion is in error. There are infinite forms of existence, and each occupies a special place in the universe — none greater or lesser than another. Labels of "better/worse", "greater/lesser", "wiser/dumber", and "more/less" set up false distinctions between the beings of earth, allowing us to think we are separate from one another.

I believe the truth is that we are a Unified Whole, emanating from, inextricably bound to, and expressing a unifying Divine Intelligence and love.

As I've mentioned, I did not always entertain this viewpoint. Growing up, throughout adulthood, and for the duration of my first marriage, and much of my second, cats and dogs were always around, but I never recognized the complexities of their makeup. To me, they were little more than animated stuffed toys, with, perhaps an instinct or two thrown in. I could not conceive of the fact that underneath that furry exterior was an intelligent, sentient being, silently watching me, and open to the potential of understanding and connecting with me.

I certainly wasn't exposed to the idea that I could interact with animals in an intelligent "conversation" between us. My empirical mind didn't even entertain the possibility. Enter Oscar, the Wonder Cat, with his bright eyes that seemed to say, "Here I am! I'm Oscar!" He even announced his name by projecting his thoughts into the quantum energy field, and presenting images to me and to the vet who "named" him. I noted earlier that while petting him, I thought of the old Oscar Mayer Wiener commercial. Later, a vet tech watched him at play and envisioned the famed boxer, Oscar De La Hoya. Both of us "thought" of the name "Oscar". In my present understanding, I am now convinced that we each came up with the name because Oscar himself was projecting it to us. Oscar made his intention known. Just because he didn't use words didn't mean that he could not convey a clear, unequivocal message. When he sent the thought "Oscar", the vet and I each built a story around that name to convince ourselves that we had thought it up on our own. This is similar to the stories I built during my early communication attempts having to do with "the boat", Sweet Pea the cat, and Cody, the horse. When

Oscar told us his name, I had absolutely no belief that animals could communicate, so the fact that the vet and I both thought of the name seemed to be a coincidence. This seemed the only possible explanation, right?

By his very being, Oscar was and is — a game changer. In an earlier chapter, I described how he came into our lives. As I was driving away from home to go to a meeting, having said goodbye to him, I was hit with an overwhelming sense that he had to stay with us. I had no concept that Oscar himself was sending me a message. I didn't know whether the message to give him a forever home was the voice of Divine Intelligence or just my gut feeling. In either case, I felt a resounding thunderbolt that I simply could not ignore.

Now that I understand our ability to communicate with all species through the quantum field and receive their communications in turn, I have no doubt that the thunderbolt was, in fact, Oscar saying, "I need to stay here." I could have ignored that message and just assumed it was a passing thought that I had created. Somehow, the feeling was so intense and the message so urgent, that something inside of me commanded me to pay attention.

Over the years, Oscar's behavior and actions have made me realize how little I knew about cats and their thought processes. Earlier I described how he came to warn us about a coyote walking outside our living room window. He didn't run away, he didn't freeze, he didn't hide; he came to tell his people.

He has also shown remarkable intelligence and forethought in how he plays. One of his favorite games is hide and seek. When he wants to play with us, he vocalizes in a distinct way, so as to alert us. Typically, he runs behind the living room curtains or jumps to the top shelf of the clothes closet, calling out, "Come find me!" Another one of his favorite games takes place when we make the bed. As soon as the top sheet goes on, Oscar burrows under it, hoping to spar and be tickled. The first time this happened, he played with his claws out, just as cats do with each other. After we explained to him that he had to keep his claws in to protect the sheets and our delicate human skin (and not injure us accidentally), he respected our wishes. He continues to always retract his claws whenever he plays with us.

Oscar is well beyond the kitten stage, yet he likes to wrestle, spar, and play with toys. I didn't even know that older cats enjoyed such activity, but he has mastered the concept of play. *How cute!* I say to myself as I watch him. I have to wonder if he thinks the same of me as I'm looking at the picture box (read: television screen), excitedly rooting for my favorite football team. "How cute my person is!"

Although he is clearly the leader cat, Oscar often chooses to yield when his brothers want to play. While busy enjoying a romp with a particular toy, Oscar may sense or spot one of the other cats looking on and wanting to play. In those instances, he frequently steps back and allows them to take turns. After a while, he will jump in again and take his turn. The concept of sharing among cats was once inconceivable to me, but now, through Oscar, I observe the behavior and realize how much I have learned from this amazing being.

Some of the most interesting interactions that I have witnessed are the ways in which Oscar plays differently with his brothers, according to their ages and abilities. His play behavior with Oliver (his peer in size, speed, and age) is full on, as they race through the house. While playing tag or wrestling with each other, they look like one big fur ball. When Obe Juan (who was much older and slower paced), came into the family Oscar would throw himself down in front of Obe and, in v-e-r-y s-l-o-w motion, invite Obe Juan to play.

Oscar is also a peacemaker. When Obe Juan first came to live with us, Oliver would sometimes engage in aggressive "stare downs" with him. On three separate occasions, Catherine and I witnessed Oscar observe the behavior, and then deliberately move from across the room to position himself between the two, and break the tension between them. Eventually, with the help of some communication with Jeri Ryan, peace was established, and Oliver and Obe became very dear friends.

Perhaps Oscar's selflessness and compassion were most evident when Obe Juan passed away. Oscar and Obe Juan both slept on our bed at night, but on different corners. The night before the vet was scheduled to come to our house and euthanize Obe, Oscar spent the night sleeping next to Obe with one paw resting on his friend. The following morning, after Obe Juan had passed away, Oscar sat near the front door as we took Obe's body to the vet's car. As we came back inside, empty handed, he gave two long, loud, mournful, wolf-like howls. He then went to his cat bed in the office, and barely moved from there for three days. Such out-of-self-awareness is a wonderful example of the capacity of animals to feel compassion, connection, love, and loss.

Oscar's new friend and protégé, Otis (our recent addition to the family) follows Oscar like the inspired leader that he is. I will write more about Otis and how he came to live with us in a following chapter. Suffice it to say here, Oscar has once again proven himself to be a wonder cat.

There is a wall hanging in our house that has a quote from the Buddha. It reads "Thousands of candles can be lighted from a single candle, and the life of the candle will not be shortened. Happiness never decreases by being shared." I can never see that quote without thinking of Oscar.

As I continue to observe Oscar, I see him as a ripple effect — the pebble that dropped into the pond and caused a stir. Because of him, I became fascinated with cats and began to study them. I have learned much and am still expanding my knowledge about the illusory animal-human divide. I have talked to countless animals and their people, and have witnessed so many humans and animals become closer and more aware of our common oneness — all because of the little tabby in the fur coat, who told the world, "I am Oscar." And so I pause to thank Oscar, the Wonder Cat, my conduit to this odyssey into the quantum field.

CHAPTER 17

ODE TO OBE JUAN, MY ZEN MASTER

How is it possible for a former die-hard empiricist to feel overwhelming grief at the loss of a spirit housed in a white furry body? How do you say "goodbye" to a soul-connection who indelibly changed your life in the brief span of four years – just by being? For me having ushered my Zen master Obe Juan, into the world of Spirit, those questions are slowly resolving themselves. Even in his passing, Obe Juan continues to be my teacher and, somehow, still helps in my evolution and understanding of the mystery of life's big questions.

My devastation at Obe Juan's death took me by surprise. After all, I was no stranger to loss, having endured the passing of my grandparents, my parents, two brothers, and other relatives and friends. I thought, therefore, that I understood the fleeting nature of temporal life, and I certainly knew that Obe Juan would not live forever. The reality was that in his last months with us, his physical health had been rapidly declining. When

Catherine and I first adopted him, our vet examined him and estimated his age to be between twelve and fourteen years. We knew that our parting would come sooner than with a younger cat, but for us, his age didn't matter. He was part of our family, and we loved him.

In Obe Juan's first medical exam, we discovered that he was afflicted by the onset of kidney failure. More than one-third of all house cats die of this problem that many believe is exacerbated by improper diet. One of the extremely important items that we learned during our initial education regarding cats was about the feeding of cats and the pet food industry. Up until about 1950, the animal feed industry had been making dog food for many, many years, but very little cat food. Most cats were like the ones I grew up with — outdoor cats who hunted for their food. For the most part, in their association with humans, cats' value to people was in hunting vermin, which would otherwise eat the human's grain crop. Therefore, bringing cats inside and providing food for them would have been counterproductive from the human standpoint.

About fifty years ago, however, people began to keep cats as pets, and now cats outnumber dogs in the American pet population. The pet food industry, seeing an opportunity for expansion, began to market cat food, but many companies used the dog food formulas they already had and added flavoring that would appeal to cats. This created a big problem for cats, for while dogs are omnivores and can eat and thrive on almost anything, cats are obligate carnivores and require a high-quality protein meat diet to thrive. Dog food has lots of grains, vegetables, and other fillers and is very light on the animal protein that cats require for proper health. One result of this deficiency is often gradual kidney failure made worse by continual subclinical dehydration. A dry food, or "kibble" diet makes this situation worse. Cats have a limited thirst mechanism and, in the wild, get most of their hydration from their prey. In the case of domestic cats, their moisture comes from canned "wet" food. Even when water is readily available, cats don't drink enough to offset their chonic low level dehydration.

In his first three years with us, Obe's health noticeably improved and then remained relatively steady; but during his fourth year, gradual deterioration became more evident. For the few months prior to his passing, Obe had difficulty walking. Catherine and I purchased some pet stairs to facilitate his navigation onto our bed, where he loved to sleep, and although he managed the steps, that was all he could do. His weak legs could no longer accommodate the jump to a chair or sofa. He developed high blood pressure, some vision problems, had difficulty moving and jumping, and exhibited intermittent confusion. Toward the end of his days, he could barely make it to the litter box. Occasionally, when he did manage to get there, he would often step in with his front paws, leaving his hind legs hanging out.

Our primary objectives became his comfort and to ease his suffering. In the early and middle stages of his physical decline, his faculties had slowly begun to fail. However, he continued to enjoy many aspects of his daily life — sunny spots to nap in, little chicken tid-bit treats, and the companionship of us and his brothers. Then, came a sudden, steep nosedive of his health and well-being. The previously theoretical discussions of the best course of action for him became painfully immediate.

In bearing witness to Obe's physical debilitation, we prepared ourselves and each other for his imminent departure from the temporal plane; but when it happened, we were sideswiped by an emotional tornado. Previously, we had spoken with a professional communicator who, after connecting with Obe Juan, confirmed that he knew his time was very near, and that he would entrust us with the decision-making process.

No one wants to face that terrible decision, but when the time came, and we felt it was in Obe's best interest that he leave his body, we decided to help him transition. We did some research and found "Paws into Grace", a local in-home euthanasia veterinary organization. With heavy hearts and great love for our teacher who, in his brief stay with us, transformed our lives forever, we made that painful call.

As had been his habit, Obe spent his last night on our bed. It was a long and sleepless night for us and we wanted to make sure he was comfortable. As previously described, Oscar stayed close to him all night, supplying warmth and comfort.

The previous two nights had been mostly sleepless for Catherine and me, as we tried to remain awake to carry Obe to the litter box. His failing legs couldn't take him very far. On his last morning after we took him to the litter box, he went into Catherine's office instead of returning to the bed. As had been his custom when there, he went to his favorite spot on the carpet in a patch of the morning sun, where he lay on his side, languidly lifting his head toward the sunlight.

When the vet entered the room, Obe Juan didn't resist but remained, as ever, undaunted by the past or future. The vet administered a sedative injection to put him into a tranquil sleep. As he dozed off, I lifted my Zen Master in my arms and held him while the vet then shaved his foreleg to find a vein. She then inserted a needle, into which the fluid would be inserted – the substance that would stop his precious heart. In those moments, I hardly knew how my own continued to beat.

As Catherine and I sat on the floor holding our dear friend, the vet administered the fluid, and Obe's spirit left his body. For about ten minutes afterward, we communicated with him in spirit, radiating pure love from our hearts and tears. This was one of the few times that I had held him for any length of time. Typically, whenever I wanted to hold Obe, he would sit for a few seconds, wiggle a little to let me know that he had received his required dose of physical affection, and leave. The longest period that I had ever held him was for about thirty minutes when I first met and sat with him in his exercise pen at a Rescue House adoption fair. His customary display of love manifested in the rubbing of his chin on my feet. He loved to be stroked and enjoyed belly rubs while he stretched out on the floor, and sometimes he liked just to be in same room, looking at us. However, being a lap cat was not Obe's style.

Above all, Obe Juan was an observer. One of his favorite pastimes was lying on the landing at the top of the stairs, at the intersection of our two offices, our bedroom, and guest bathroom. It was a great place to keep track of goings-on both up and downstairs while making himself available for belly rubs as we passed by. He never commented or meowed except for one memorable trip home from the vet's, when he vocalized incessantly after a tooth extraction. Other than that time, I can probably count on one hand the number of times I heard him speak.

Meows are cats' method of communicating with humans. When cats communicate with each other, they use intuitive communication, body language, and other vocalizations (they have about one hundred different choices of sound). Obe didn't feel the need to express himself verbally to us humans. Even so, Catherine and I were always amazed that although Obe was the quietest being we had ever known, he continually radiated a sense of profound presence. He simply maintained a calm demeanor at all times, always aware of his place in the Divine Order. Panic was not his way of being in the world. Even a loud vacuum cleaner (which he clearly did not like) was nothing more than an object to avoid. Therefore, when we turned on that offensive noisemaker, he calmly left the room.

Obe's Zen essence was at no time more evident than when we had to administer subcutaneous fluids as part of his ongoing treatment for kidney failure. The process was similar to rudimentary dialysis, designed to add fluid to Obe's system, causing increased urination and blood filtering. The treatment (which extended his life and made him feel considerably better) involved the insertion of a hypodermic needle in the scruff between his shoulder blades. This allowed one hundred cc's of saline solution to drip into his body in about five minutes time.

The first time I inserted the needle, he wiggled a bit and wanted to get away. I was definitely more anxious than he was. Catherine wisely advised me to remain calm and send out a positive mental image or message, so that Obe would pick up that energy ("This is going to help you. We love you and are so grateful that we can help you to feel better. You'll feel so good after your blood has been properly filtered!"). And so he did. Administering the healing fluids every other day became a matter of course, and Obe Juan was a fantastic patient. When I would heat up the bag of hydration fluid (by allowing it to sit in a sink of hot water) and place a towel under him, he never once squirmed or complained. Sometimes, he curled up outside the bathroom and patiently waited while I prepared the drip. At other times, when he wanted to temporarily avoid the procedure, he retreated to his "Cat Cave" under the dining room table — an area that we, and even Oscar and Oliver, respected as a sanctuary. Sooner or later, he would decide that he was ready, and come out to receive his fluids.

In his short time with us, Obe Juan taught me many lessons and conferred so much joy. Through him I learned a quiet appreciation of the All, of Presence, and of Being. He left me that legacy, and I continue the ongoing journey of living in the now, in a state of gratitude. I am still learning that it is not necessary to react emotionally to everything that happens in life. When I resort to that very human behavior, I try to pause, put the situation in perspective, and ask myself, *What would Obe Juan do?*

More than anything, the most difficult challenge for me, in the wake of my Zen Master's transition into even higher consciousness, is dealing with the pain occasioned by his physical absence. I firmly believe that his soul essence has transitioned to a different form and that his intellect and individuality are present in the quantum field. I continue to communicate with him, as I have with other animals who have transitioned. Despite this intellectual knowledge and practical experience, I still miss his physical presence.

Marta Williams' advice in her book, *Ask Your Animal*, provides solace and insight:

"The kind of relationship we have with an animal is more profound than anything possible with another human because animals have qualities humans do not. They inhabit the present moment completely, in mind, body, and spirit, bringing us with them away from our focus on the future and the past. When we can join an animal in that present-tense world, time stands still; and life completely involves us."

And so we bade farewell to the physical manifestation of Obe Juan, a quintessential Guardian of the Present, who taught me so very much and asked for nothing in return. As for goodbyes, well, at the zero-point energy of the quantum field, there is no need for such because there is only continuance. As I held him my arms while his spirit left his body, I wanted to say more, but then I realized that in life as in death, Obe Juan transcended expression. I could only breathe, "Thank you, thank you, thank you."

OBE JUAN

CHAPTER 18

THE ODYSSEY CONTINUES

After Obe Juan had transitioned, Catherine and I did not think about adopting another cat. The wounds of grief were still very new, and the high-maintenance care of our beloved Zen Master had left us ready for a break. A two-cat household seemed quite nice, and we had no plans to change that. Little did we know what Divine Order had in store for us.

I continued to communicate with various friends' animals, and with animals referred to me by word of mouth. I also would occasionally communicate with cats who were in the Rescue House system awaiting adoption. One day I received a call from Lauren, the Rescue House foster care coordinator, asking if I would talk to two cats she had in her care. I agreed and prepared to talk with Otis and Fiera, expecting nothing more than a casual conversation.

Lauren sent me pictures of the two cats and explained that Otis had a birth defect that prevented him from having full use of his back legs. His hind legs did not bend at the knee or ankle. The evaluation that he underwent at the vet for the Rescue House didn't reveal a definitive cause for his condition. It appeared that his ligaments or tendons were frozen in place, so there was no flex in his legs, and the bones were pulled at unnatural angles to each other.

Otis was shy and hesitant, and in the picture Lauren sent me his underdeveloped legs stuck straight out in front of him when he sat down. All I knew was that Otis's disability prevented him from walking, running, and jumping in the so-called "conventional" feline sense. He walked with something akin to a John Wayne swagger, because, to swing his back legs forward when he walked, he had to swivel his hips. While at Lauren's house, Otis had been bullied by a couple of the other cats, and was in need of a peaceful, forever home.

When I spoke to Otis, he was cautious but he had one of the brightest and cheeriest dispositions I have ever observed in a cat. "You'll be taken care of," I told him, "but you have to do your part by sending out the proper vibrations when looking for your person. Look at people, make a decision, and let them know how you feel." Immediately, I received the reply, "What about you?" I was so taken aback by his comment and the upbeat, happy manner in which he said it, that I laughed out loud. I had never had an animal say this to me before.

Catherine and I talked it over and thought long and hard, but we were just not ready yet for a new family member. Still, there was something about Otis that drew me to him, and a week after our initial conversation, I went to meet him in person at Lauren's house. There he was, in a little cat cave, reticent and unsure. I went over, petted and spoke with him. It was quite clear he was a beautiful spirit with a wonderful disposition and outlook on life. After visiting with him two more times, I was most definitely enamored by the charming, sweet soul with his unique mode of ambulation. However, I couldn't stop wondering if he could navigate the stairs in our home. *How can he push off of his back legs to climb, or balance to come down?* I wondered. It seemed impossible. Yet, I felt compelled to foster him. At least, we could let him explore our terrain and see what happened.

When Otis first graced our home with his presence, we isolated him in Catherine's office for a twenty-four period, so that he could acclimate to his new surroundings without immediately having to face strange cats. After a day, we put Oscar and Oliver in the bedroom and let Otis out to explore the house. At that time, he didn't navigate the stairs at all; he just ambled in the hallway between our offices. Then, slowly, the integration progress began, and one at a time, we allowed Oscar and Oliver into the office to meet Otis. The introduction went well. Otis went over to each of the boys, touched noses and purred, and they did the same. As most cats are wont to do, they sniffed one another all over, showed proper cat etiquette in their body language, and were quite satisfied with each other. Within two weeks, we signed the adoption papers. Otis was ours, and we were his.

OTIS

After just a few weeks, our new family member had fit right into the fold. He worships the ground Oscar walks on and wants to play non-stop. As for his restrictions, he doesn't seem to realize that he has any. Despite my initial concerns, the staircase doesn't pose the formidable obstacle at all. When he climbs the stairs, Otis puts his front paws on the step ahead of him. He then leans forward to put his weight on his front legs, and uses the muscles in his back to lift up his entire back end, and place his hind legs right behind his front ones. He repeats this process all the way up. When he descends, he just flies down using his front paws and leaving his hind legs to their own devices. He climbs to the top of all four of the differently styled cat trees in the house by hooking his front paws on the next highest platform, then dragging or lifting his hindquarters up behind him. He is truly amazing to watch!

One of the more interesting parts of Otis' integration was how he attached himself to Oscar and followed him around day and night. One day Catherine and I observed Oscar going through the pet door to the enclosed patio while Otis looked on in obvious confusion. Otis' body language and mannerisms spoke volumes. "How did Oscar go through that wall?" Obviously the wheels were turning, but he would not be left behind. Mustering up his courage, he bravely tried the pet door and discovered the mechanics of it. Once on the "catio", Otis waited a few minutes, looked around and began to pace. "Now that I'm here, how do I get back?" he seemed to say. Oscar, who usually stays for long periods on the catio, looked at him for a long moment, and seeing his concern, calmly walked over and used the door to come back inside. This was a clear example of Oscar's mentorship and an "a-ha" moment for Otis. He learned the mechanics of the pet door "inside out" you might say and now freely uses the pet door to go outside and enjoy the fresh air.

As he did with Obe Juan, Oscar also uses a different speed to play with Otis. He even has made the decision not to run up and down the stairs when playing chase, as Otis moves much more slowly there than on level floors.

Just as Obe Juan was my Zen master, Otis is my hero. Recently, I read a quote by the late actor, author, and activist, Christopher Reeve (1952-2004). After becoming famous for playing Superman in the movies, Reeve was injured in a horse riding accident and paralyzed from the neck down. He devoted the rest of his life to raising money for spinal cord injury research. He was often called a hero for his tireless effort.

His response was, "I think a hero is an ordinary individual who finds the strength to persevere and endure in spite of overwhelming obstacles." Otis fits that description. It is an absolute joy to see him climbing on cat trees and chasing his mouse on a string. He may be "different", but his uniqueness makes him who he is — and we wouldn't want him to be anything other than his authentic self.

And the odyssey continues. Two months after Otis came to live with us, another being of the four-legged variety showed up in our lives. Our trusted cat-sitter Ernie found a young orange tabby cat roaming around his neighborhood, emaciated, ragged, abandoned and alone in the country. Apparently, his humans had moved and left him behind, leaving him to fend for himself. Ernie realized that the poor guy had been abandoned and began feeding him when he came to his house. Ernie was not in a position to keep this starving, friendly cat, so he called my daughter Trace and me to tell us about the cat that he had found. Trace told Ernie to set a cat trap, capture it, and then take it to the vet. The vet would then get the cat into the Rescue House system.

After trapping him and dropping him off at the vet, Ernie came straight to our house and asked us if we would be willing to foster him. Ernie, as you may remember, is a family member whom we deeply respect, admire, and love. After telling us about this wonderful and friendly cat, we could not resist. When the vet called to say that he had been neutered, microchipped, de-fleaed and inoculated, we picked him up and brought him home. After trying several different names, and getting no indication from the cat himself, we decided on "Oberto", which signifies nobility and light.

The process of integrating Oberto into our family was far different than anything I have previously experienced. After a year with us, Oberto had not fully adapted, and he could not be in the same room with the other cats. We followed the same protocol of keeping the cats apart for the first few days, but when we introduced them to each other, there was instant tension. Oberto had been abandoned and forced to survive on his own in the country while competing with other feral cats for food. In his experience, other cats were not friends, they were competitors. Accordingly, when he saw any other cat (e.g., Oscar and Oliver), he sensed an immediate threat. Otis did not interact with Oberto, as he seemed to want to stay well clear of the newcomer. Oscar and Oliver could sense Oberto's defensiveness and fear and hence, the attempted integration process was characterized by confrontation, intimidation and challenging stare- downs.

OBERTO

This was not what I had planned. On two occasions, both of which occurred when Catherine was away for a couple of days, Oberto managed to slip out of his room and he and Oscar got into huge fights. I immediately called Lisa Larson, who spoke with all of the boys. Oscar was entirely against the idea of Oberto coming to live with us. This was his territory, and he wanted to retain the Lead Feline Guardian role. Oberto indicated that he wanted to stay with us, but he wanted to be left alone and not deal with other cats. Lisa described him as actually being in a state of post-traumatic stress after having been abandoned and forced to live in survival mode to stay alive in the wilderness.

Over a period of months, we slowly continued to introduce the boys to each other. One tactic we used was to set up a baby gate between rooms and feed cat treats to the group while they were in sight of each other and could have a positive experience while in close proximity. Oscar, Oliver, and Otis would be on one side of the gate, and Oberto on the other. At first, Oberto would go to the far side of the room and turn his back on the others. Gradually, over the course of months, he moved closer and closer, until eventually they were all nose to nose, enjoying their treats.

Oberto has changed tremendously during his time with us and is a truly wonderful cat. Cautious at first, he has become a very friendly, affectionate companion who purrs instantly when petted, and really takes to humans. He and his brothers are still acclimating, and their relationships continue to get friendlier. To his credit, our newest addition did virtually everything that we have asked of him. Early in his stay with us, he failed to use the litter box on one occasion. I explained that he had to conform to that practice, as he was no longer outdoors in the countryside. He was in a home and had to abide by indoor cat rules. He understood, and never transgressed again.

To illustrate another example, when Oberto was petted along his back, initially he would roll over on his back and go into a defensive mode, with legs up and all claws out — a standard cat fighting tactic. "I'm not a threat to you," I told him. "My tender human skin will be shredded by your claws. So, you have to keep your claws in when interacting with me." He took a while, but has gradually relaxed and is now very careful to keep his claws in and to be careful of my skin.

Admittedly, all of the feline tumult and acrimony was very damaging to my ego. Why couldn't I stop or change the situation? Why weren't the boys listening to me and following my plan? Were my animal communication skills not working? The reality is I am learning that I still have a lot to learn. Animal communication does not mean animal coercion. Each entity has a personality — a complex emotional and psychological presence, and a destiny. I can help and facilitate, but I cannot direct and dictate.

There is a famous Zen *koan* that is appropriate to my circumstances: "When the student is ready, the teacher will appear." I am so grateful that Oberto has appeared in my life to teach more of the lessons that I need and want to learn…and the Odyssey continues!

CHAPTER 19

CHANGING THE WORLD

Every seismic shift in consciousness begins with a small group of dedicated individuals. American anthropologist Margaret Mead (1901-1978) posited that it only takes a small group of people to change the world. She continues on with her belief that such small groups are the only thing that has changed the world. When I contemplate her thoughts and the truth behind them, I cannot help but feel a sense of hope and optimism for the future. I do not know if Ms. Mead had a spiritual or metaphysical basis for her thoughts but for me, her statement embraces the fact that we are all part of the Divine Order, intricately connected as one. As more people come to acknowledge the Divine Truth of the oneness of all life, the deceptive, human-created notion that one group of individuals is "better", "greater", and "superior" or, conversely "lesser than", "subordinate", or "inferior to" must, in its various forms, fade from the human psyche.

I once attended a talk by Episcopalian theologian Bishop John Shelby Spong in which he stated that once a topic of conversation concerning social change finds its way into open dialogue, the discussed change is inevitable. As a few people or a few small groups begin to question the validity of an established paradigm, the questions start a discussion about new ideas. Eventually, if the new ideas "have legs" (as the saying goes), it is only a matter of time until they work their way into the general populace. After that, the change inevitably occurs. Bishop Spong did not make reference to Margaret Mead or quote her, but in my opinion, his thoughts are very similar and for me, convey the same idea.

I believe that the awareness of the role of animals in our world and the importance of their place in the universe is entering human consciousness to a greater degree, and this awareness will continue to grow. Because of a small group of dedicated people, humanity will come to realize that all living things have importance and that the lives of all beings are intertwined. Not only are our lives intertwined, but according to noted astrophysicist Neil deGrasse Tyson, we are all made of the same stuff. In his TV series, *The Cosmos*, which was an updated version of a series first done by Carl Sagan, Dr. Tyson explains how the few basic elements that combine to make stars are the same ones that are the building blocks of all life. These elements radiate out from stars, congregate on planets, and eventually evolve into life. According to Sagan and Tyson, we are all the same, and we are all made of "star stuff".

As I mentioned at the beginning of this book, human consciousness is, in fact, ever changing. Just one hundred fifty-five years ago slavery was approved and condoned by our government as the law of the land. Now it is illegal in every country in the world. After many generations of work, the woman's suffrage movement culminated in 1920 with the passage of the Nineteenth Amendment to the U.S. Constitution, giving women the right to vote. Same-gender rights are also evolving. The Supreme Court has now recognized marriage equality as a fundamental right, and same gender marriage is now nationally recognized. These are all huge shifts is social consciousness which indicate how humans are continually evolving.

I firmly believe that the concepts of animal rights, animal communication, and thought-energy transmission within the quantum field are increasingly becoming an accepted reality. I believe that the false notion that we humans are greater than or superior to other beings in the universe is not accurate. We may have different ways of living and surviving in the world — and that is fine, but in the overall design of life, each living being has value, importance, and purpose. On many levels, the interconnectedness of the web of all life is becoming more apparent with the awareness that what affects one species will sooner or later affect all.

Practices such as using animals for cosmetic testing, and even medical testing, can and should be eliminated. Factory farming, fur farming, and all forms of animal fighting for entertainment such as cock, dog, and bullfighting, should be illegal. These actions relegate animals to a lesser and unimportant status and create absolutely unnecessary suffering. It is my hope that these practices, which some people presently consider to be acceptable, will soon be recognized as abhorrent.

Small groups of concerned citizens have been working to initiate these changes, and the influence of many of these groups continues to grow. The first of animal rights groups in this country was the American Society for the Prevention of Cruelty to Animals (ASPCA), founded in 1866. Their primary focus was to end cockfighting and the unregulated nature of slaughterhouses. The National Anti-Vivisection Society was founded in England in 1875 in order to end the exploitation of animals used in science. The Humane Society of the United States (HSUS) was founded in 1954 with the purpose of ending animal fighting and the using of animals for testing. People for the Ethical Treatment of Animals (PETA), founded in 1980, specifically focused on the abuses of factory farming and fur farming. Organizations such as these are on the leading edge of changing the dialogue about the place of animals in the world. Compared to the thousands of years humans have been on the earth, they are all relative newcomers in the world but are making a huge impact on shifting the paradigm of how we view animals.

Albert Schweitzer (1875-1965), winner of the 1952 Nobel Peace Prize, was noted for his philosophy of "Reverence for Life". In his Nobel Prize acceptance speech, he said "Compassion in which ethics takes root does not assume its true proportions until it embraces not only man, but every living being."

Of course, humans have been using animals as a food source since our species evolved. For much of the world, throughout history and still today, animal meat is a supplement to the diet and not a primary source of protein. Plant-based protein has been proven to be entirely adequate for human nutrition and recent nutritional studies have shown plant based diets to be superior to meat based diets for many measures of health indicators. As a vegetarian for many years, I have run marathons, practiced martial arts, and hiked through the Peruvian Andes for many days, all fueled by plant protein. Considering the high environmental costs of raising livestock, and the absolutely horrendous conditions in which much of our livestock is forced to live, I think it is essential that in order for our species to survive, we will have to stop eating other animals.

Change can be a long and slow process, but once started, can proceed rapidly. It was not until the 1950's that books on animal communication began to appear on bookshelves. Now, in the early twenty-first century, there are numerous books on the topic, along with seminars, training sessions, YouTube videos and movies. The people who read about, study, and practice animal communication are a relatively small group of thoughtful, committed citizens. However, they are growing in number, and animal communication is a topic of conversation, working its way into human consciousness.

Quantum physicists have proven that thoughts create measurable energy that then become part of the quantum field. These quanta of energy can be received and accessed by others which means that perhaps, eventually, language as we humans know it will not be necessary for communication. In turn, the idea that animals can hear us, receive our messages, and communicate with us, will revolutionize the world. We will come to realize that we humans are not the sole guardians of Earth, but that all life forms have a purpose and have the right to fulfill that purpose.

In the reality of the quantum energy field, all beings have access to the thought-energy at the zero-point energy of the field. We only have to send out our energy to be heard, and *listen* to receive responses. Our thoughts are like waves that are transmitted to other living entities in the quantum field. Other beings of all species are capable of tapping into the field and exchanging intelligent thoughts with us and with each other. All we have to do is ask, and the conversation has begun. I have never spoken to an animal who didn't answer "yes" to the question, "May I talk to you?"

Once we begin to shift our awareness and acknowledge that we live in the quantum energy field, we will find the world to be a much more expansive place. That spider on the window sill has awareness, feelings and a will to survive, just like we humans do. It just lives in a different manner, with different priorities and motivations. These are no less important to its life than our priorities and motivations are to each of us. Many might act on impulse and snuff out the life of a fellow being without a second thought. In reality that spider's life is as valuable to him as my life is to me. We are all made of the same "star stuff", we all exist in the quantum field, and we all have awarenesses, thoughts, feelings and a will to live.

I'm reminded of the story in which a tourist goes out to the beach after a very high tide and sees thousands of starfish stranded on the sand, about to die. The tourist observes a beachcomber walking along, and after every two or three steps, the beachcomber picks up a starfish and throws it back into the water. The tourist goes up to the beachcomber and inquires, "What are you doing? There are thousands of starfish here. There's no way that you can pick all of them up and throw them back. You can't possibly make a difference here." The beachcomber bends down, picks up another starfish, tosses it into the water, looks at the tourist and calmly says, "It makes a difference to that one."

Every day, each one of us can make a difference — one thought, one smile, one word of understanding, one loving gesture at a time. As you embark on your own odyssey into the quantum field, you will be amazed at how profound, and numerous the changes within yourself will be. You will also produce changes in other sentient, intelligent beings around you — and the world-at-large. Take the leap and discover how far-reaching your impact will be, and never, ever doubt — even for a moment — how a small group of thoughtful, committed citizens can change the world.

Epilogue

In closing, I thought that it would be fitting to include the thoughts, words, and feelings of one of the precious sentient beings in my life, our little black cat, Oliver. In that little being lies the wisdom of the universe. In fact, he is a microcosm who represents the "stuff" of the stars, and he certainly encapsulates, in his very being and essence, the ideas expressed in this writing.

In the course of our communications with Dr. Jeri Ryan, one of my most fascinating lessons was that animals sometimes compose poetry. This came to light because, in one of her conversations with Oliver, she informed us that he recited a poem that had come into his mind — yes, a poem!

Allow me to set the scene. Jeri has never been in our or Oliver's physical presence, and she has neither visited us nor seen our home in photographs. In our living room, there is a big picture window with small vent windows at the bottom to allow the breeze to come in, frequently causing the living room drapes to billow. Just off our master bedroom, we have a small screened-in balcony with a pet door, which allows the cats to enjoy the outdoors. Oliver loves to sit out there at night. The following poem expresses his awareness and state of at-oneness with all beings:

Curtains blowing in the breeze
      Bring peace and gentleness inside.
Then we can have even more
      Peace and gentleness.
Curtains blowing in the breeze
      Bring special peace and gentleness inside.
Let's look at the stars too.
They make life very big,
      Even bigger than we think it is,
Because life is spread all over you know.
And that's what stars do.
They tell us that,
      And they spread it too.

I am a work in process, still filled with a sense of awe and wonder about the process of speaking with other species. The "real world", as I thought I knew it, is not the world I know and live in today. As with all life, I am sure I will continue to evolve and change, for that is the nature of life. I continue to be eternally grateful to Oscar, that beautiful soul in a cat body, who started me on this path. I am also grateful to another mystic soul in a fur body, Oliver, who emphasized to me "Life is bigger than we think it is." It is certainly much, much bigger than I thought it was.

Oh, Oliver! You sure got that right!

Appendix A

QUANTUM WEIRDNESS AND ZERO-POINT ENERGY FIELD

There is an old "down home" country saying that goes: "If you have to swallow a bunch of live frogs, it's best to swallow the biggest one first." With that thought in mind of swallowing "the biggest one first", let's talk about quantum weirdness and the zero-point energy field.

First, some perspective. If I had lived a thousand years ago, I would have thought the earth was flat, and the sun came up from the ground every day and sank back in again every night. My modern, sophisticated self knows the earth is a sphere, and it orbits around the sun. However, in my daily life, I still experience the earth as flat, and even though I know better, I say the sun rises and sets.

In his book, *The Cosmic Code: Quantum Physics as the Language of Nature*[xv], Heinz R Pagels coins the term "quantum weirdness". He uses this very non-technical term to illustrate how quantum physics is so counter to the Newtonian physics upon which started the industrial revolution. He puts it this way: "In the quantum theory...common sense interpretations of the world cannot be maintained...It is meaningless to speak of a quantum particle such as an electron resting at a point in space. Furthermore, electrons can materialize in places where Newton's laws say they can't be. Physicists and mathematicians have shown that thinking about quantum particles as ordinary objects is in conflict with experiment."

The weirdness of the quantum world is that physicists have found that everything we think of as solid matter is not matter at all. *Everything* is energy. As scientists delved into what was thought to be the smallest particles in the universe, atoms, they found even smaller sub-atomic particles, to which they gave names like quarks, bosons, leptons, and neutrinos. As they broke down these sub-atomic particles, they discovered something weird. What they thought was matter is wave energy. But not all the time. Sometimes these particles are matter, and sometimes they are waves of energy.

Even though in my ordinary everyday life I think of everything as solid matter, it is not. I still sit in chairs, eat food, drive cars and interact with people, but all of those seemingly solid things are, at the very basic sub-atomic level, energy. Each person, animal, and plant - all living things - are bundles or quanta of energy.

I have used the analogy before of the quantum field as an ocean. All living things are like waves in this ocean. We are all individual waves, but still all part of, and made up of, the ocean. If we go below the surface of the ocean, we can go to a depth at which the energy of our individual wave dissipates and is joined with the energy of the entire ocean. This is akin to what is known as the zero-point energy - the place where our individual energies meld with that of all living things.

It may seem weird to think everything is energy. It may also seem strange to know we are all connected to everything. However, this is no more strange than to have looked at a beautiful sunset a thousand years ago and think of the spherical earth spinning on its axis as it orbits the sun. It is all a matter of perspective.

END NOTES

i   *Gerald G. Jampolsky: Love is Letting go of Fear, Celestial Arts, 2004, ISBN 1587611962*

ii   *Stephen Cope: The Great Work of your Life, Bantam, 2012, ISBN 9780553807516*

iii *Sun Tzu: The Art of War, Nabla, 2010, ISBN 1936276011*

iv *J. Allen Boone: Kinship with all Life, Harper One, 1976, ISBN 0060609125*

v   *Amelia Kinkade: The Language of Miracles, New World Library, 2006, ISBN 978-1577315100*

vi *Judy Meyer: The Animal Connection, Penguin Putnam, Inc., 2000 ISBN 0452281714*

vii *Eckhart Tolle: The Power of Now, Namaste Publishing, 2004, ISBN 1577314808*

viii *Michael A. Singer: The Untethered Soul, New Harbinger Publications, 2007, ISBN 1572245379*

ix *Marta Williams: Ask Your Animal, New World Library, 2008, ISBN 1577316091*

x   *Lynn McTaggart: The Field: The Quest for the Secret Force of the Universe, Harper Perennial, 2008 ISBN 006143518X*

xi *Lynn McTaggart: The Intention Experiment, Atria Books, 2008, ISBN 0743276965*

xii *Cesar Millan: Cesar's Way, Three Rivers Press, 2007, ISBN 0307337979*

xiii Jackson Galaxy: Cat Daddy, Jeremy P. Tarcher, 2013, ISBN 0399163808

xiv *Karen Pryor: Reaching the Animal Mind, Scribner, 2009, ISBN 9780743297776*

xv *Heinz Pagels: The Cosmic Code: Quantum Physics as the Language of Nature, Dover Publications, 2012, ISBN 0486485064*

Printed in the United States
By Bookmasters